The (Im)possible Multicultural Teacher

The (Im)possible Multicultural Teacher

A Critical Approach to Understanding White Teachers' Multicultural Work

Foreword by H. Richard Milner IV

Charise Pimentel
Texas State University, USA

SENSE PUBLISHERS
ROTTERDAM/BOSTON/TAIPEI

A C.I.P. record for this book is available from the Library of Congress.

ISBN: 978-94-6351-144-5 (paperback)
ISBN: 978-94-6351-145-2 (hardback)
ISBN: 978-94-6351-146-9 (e-book)

Published by: Sense Publishers,
P.O. Box 21858,
3001 AW Rotterdam,
The Netherlands
https://www.sensepublishers.com/

Cover photograph by Brian Blackwell Photography

Printed on acid-free paper

TABLE OF CONTENTS

TABLE OF CONTENTS

FOREWORD

Charise Pimentel's *The (Im)possible Multicultural Teacher: A Critical Approach to Understanding White Teachers' Multicultural Work* is a welcome addition to the teacher education literature. This is a powerful book – sure to advance what we know about the preparation of teachers to meet the needs of students who are most grossly underserved in schools across the U.S. What are particularly noteworthy about this book are the (1) explicit links between theory and practice made throughout the book; (2) scholarly, yet accessible writing approach of the author; (3) vividly rich case studies that illuminate real teachers' practices at the elementary, middle, and high school level; (4) careful attention to micro-level realities of teachers and schools, and (5) analyses of macro-level systems that advance or stifle school success. Consistent with scholarship that complicates the work of teachers and teaching for social justice, Pimentel reminds readers that teachers have the potential to reinforce as well as challenge social justice and the status quo in schools. But what is especially refreshing throughout this book is an underlying message that teachers' justice work tends not to fall in some neatly packaged binary where they are either "for" equity or "against" it in practice. But rather, disposition work of teachers as they work to become critical multicultural practitioners is much more nuanced than what a polarized way of thinking about equity for practice might suggest.

Drawing from a case study methodological approach, the book showcases the work of three White teachers: Mr. Potts, Ms. DeGraw, and Megan. Although different, each of these teachers is committed to enacting multicultural education in their classrooms and schools. Indeed, Pimentel explains that "teachers' multicultural practices, even when they put forth their best efforts, are necessarily conflicted and incoherent, rather than static assemblages of pure pedagogical practices." Especially for those teachers learning how to teach in pre-service teacher education programs, the struggles of teachers in the cases allows for spaces to understand how successful pedagogical practices are a consequence of teachers' own learning, reflection and development over time. Moreover, the cases demonstrate how teacher learning is constantly evolving and dynamic and never (should) end. Thus, in many ways, the book gives teachers *permission to develop* – to *Start Where They are* – as they work against what can be considered the grain of maintaining inequity, racism, discrimination and other forms of the status quo.

In addition, conceptually, the book provides powerful analytic principles in explaining teacher disposition orientations that can in fact be dangerous for too many students who are underserved in school. These students include but are not limited to: Black and Brown students, students whose first language is not English, Muslim students, Jewish students, immigrant students, students with ability differences, LBGQT+ students, and students who live below the poverty line.

Pimentel describes The Detached Teacher – where the emphases of curriculum, assessment, and instructional practice are on the student population with the majority presence in a school or community. A second descriptor of teachers with a problematic disposition is The Deficit Thinker – where educators "blame the victim" for their academic and social challenges and focus on what students do not possess instead of the many strengths that they do have. And the Rugged Multicultural Teacher – describes teachers who focus on themselves as the hero as an individual who will 'save' those students who tend to be underserved in schools. Of course, each of these dispositions is troublesome, and this book allows teachers to identify features of such practices, mindsets, and educator with special attention placed on how to disrupt and work through them.

Thus, as we continue to grapple with and work through a schooling and sociopolitical landscape that are indeed "anti-immigrant, anti-bilingual, and pro-White American," this book is a must read for any of us committed to supporting teachers to realize and reach their full capacity to develop and enact learning opportunities that are emancipatory and concurrently transformative. This book pushes the boundaries of what we know and do in the preparation of teachers for racial and social justice. I strongly recommend and endorse it.

H. Richard Milner IV
Helen Faison Professor of Urban Education
University of Pittsburgh

DEDICATION

I dedicate this book to my bilingual, bicultural, and biracial family: Octavio, Quetzin, Quetzalli, and Maya Pimentel. As a family, we collectively fight the Eurocentric and English monolingual school and social system, and like the work of the teachers featured in this book, this process is anything but straightforward. Our family provides me both the strength and insight to relentlessly seek social justice in not only our personal and public lives, but for all those who continue to be underserved in a racist and English language elitist educational and social system. Octavio—thank you for providing me a solid foundation to raise our family and teaching me to prioritize what matters most. Also, thank you for your ongoing support for pursuing critical projects and reaching my personal best. Quetzin, Quetzalli, and Maya—you provide me purpose. This work is as much about your own schooling experiences as it is about the hope you hold for the future. Young critical scholars yourselves, you have already proven your critical perspectives and desires to create a more just world. As you continue to grow into young adults, I will relish the distinct, but purposeful directions your lives will take. I am so proud to be your mom.

INTRODUCTION

U.S. society is plagued with racial injustices, and the schooling experiences of children, are no exception to this reality. Whether implicit or explicit, intentional or unintentional, individual or institutional—racism has been a constant in U.S. schooling experiences and outcomes. Countless educational scholars have documented and brought attention to the racial inequities in schools, signifying these schooling experiences and outcomes with terminology such as: The Chicana/ Chicano Educational Pipeline (Yosso, 2006), Subtractive Schooling (Valenzuela, 1999), Stolen Education (Alemán, 2013), the School to Prison Pipeline (Laura, 2014), and The Achievement Gap (Valencia, 2015)—to name just a few.

No doubt, teachers play a central role in students' educational experiences, and in extension, the racial equity issues students face in schools. While it may be debatable exactly how much input and what impact teachers have on designing educational programs, curricula, policies, and even pedagogical practices, most scholars agree that teachers do have the potential to reinforce as well as challenge the racial status quo in schools. As Freire (1985; 2000) has made clear, no teaching act is politically neutral. Further, White teachers in particular, whether they realize it or not, have a significant stake in racial educational equity issues. White teachers not only represent 82 percent of the teaching work force (National Center for Education Statistics, 2013), but they are ultimately the benefactors of the racial inequities that emanate from schools and the larger society. Thus, what White teachers do in their classrooms and schools to address racial inequities has the potential to not only alter the social positioning of their students of color, but their own social positioning as well.

Even with their own social standing at stake, I believe it is fair to say that most White teachers are in favor of educational equity. Indeed, it would be difficult to find a White teacher who openly admits that s/he does not want all her/his students to achieve, regardless of their students' diverse circumstances, identities, and backgrounds. With this being said, I venture to say that most White teachers are roughly working from the same educational equity goal: All students should have an equal opportunity to achieve in school. However, having the same educational equity goal does not mean that teachers' methods for realizing such a goal are the same. To the contrary, teachers' approaches to addressing educational racial inequities, and the overall effectiveness of their methods, vary widely (Banks & McGee, 2013; Sleeter & Grant, 2009).

Multicultural education scholars, for example, have brought attention to the fact that teachers do not work from a monolithic definition of multicultural education and not all approaches to multicultural education yield educational equity (Banks & McGee, 2013; Lee, Menkart, & Okazawa-Rey, 2008; Nieto & Bode, 2012; Ramsey, 2015; Sleeter & Grant, 2009). From this work, we see that some of the most popular approaches to multicultural education actually do little to transform racial inequities in schools. Among the most popular is the celebratory approach to multicultural education, whereby teachers promote educational equity for their diverse students by celebrating superficial characterizations of culture and cultural artifacts, such as food, dress, and dance (Lee, Menkart, & Okazawa-Rey, 2008; Nieto & Bode, 2012). Lee et al. (2008) point out that educators working from this celebratory approach often do little to alter a Eurocentric curriculum, beyond highlighting certain "multicultural" heroes and holidays. Rightly so, Nieto and Bode (2012) refer to this superficial and safe conception of multicultural education as "fairyland multicultural education" (p. 4). In a similar fashion, Banks and McGee (2013) critique what they call the "contributions approach", which is characterized by educators simply adding in diverse references and readings to an already whitestream (Urietta, 2009) curriculum. Needless to say, these approaches to multicultural education are ineffective because they fail to address the complex social and historical power relations that penetrate our school systems, promote racial ideologies, and reinforce racial inequities. Simply put, celebratory and contribution approaches to multicultural education fail to address the sociopolitical context of schooling. The sociopolitical context of schooling, according to Nieto and Bode (2012), refers to the constellation of "laws, regulations, policies, practices, traditions, and ideologies" (p. 4) that create inequitable power relations and give rise to not only racism, but also linguicism, sexism, classism, religious oppression, heterosexism, ableism, among other forms of oppression.

If educators truly want to achieve educational equity, they must confront and challenge the aspects of schooling that give rise to racial inequities (Banks & McGee, 2013; Milner, 2015; Nieto, 2010; Nieto, 2017; Nieto & Bode, 2012; Ramsey, 2015). That is, educators must work from a critical multicultural perspective. This calls for a transformative approach to education, whereby educators actively attempt to transform foundational aspects of schooling, including but not limited to, the curriculum, pedagogy, assessment practices, language policies and programs, disciplinary policies, and class size (Milner, 2015; Nieto & Bode, 2012). While there is a clear call for teachers to work from a critical multicultural perspective, it is not clear what critical multicultural teachers are able to achieve in school and social settings that structurally and ideologically uphold the racial status quo. In an effort to address this query, the purpose of this book is to examine what transformative possibilities lie specifically in the transformative pedagogical practices of White teachers who work from a critical multicultural perspective. With this goal in mind, this book takes readers into the classrooms of Mr. Potts, Ms. DeGraw, and Megan— three critical multicultural, White teachers who teach at elementary, middle, and high school levels. Within the case-study chapters in this book (chapters 2, 3, and 4), I detail these teachers' specific pedagogical practices, and in doing so, reveal that even despite their best intentions, the teachers' critical multicultural practices are not always transformative. That is, even though the teachers featured in this book work from a critical multicultural perspective and do create many possibilities for transforming the racial status quo in their classrooms and schools, they also encounter many pedagogical impossibilities. From these teachers' critical multicultural practices, I advance the concept of the (im)possible multicultural teacher.

Before I jump into the specific case-study chapters that highlight the teachers' contradictory practices, I must first conceptualize the idea of the (im)possible multicultural teacher. I do so in the following sections of this chapter by differentiating the (im)possible multicultural teacher among other common teaching dispositions that often emerge when teachers think about, rationalize, and confront the racial achievement gap. According to Mercado (2016), teaching dispositions "are the engines that drive capacities related to knowledge and skills, and these are especially significant when it comes to working with children and youth from marginalized communities" (p. 28). The teaching dispositions I discuss in this chapter include: The Detached Teacher, The Deficit Thinker, The Rugged Multicultural Teacher, and the (Im)possible Multicultural Teacher. These teaching dispositions are not necessarily approaches to multicultural education (Banks & McGee, 2013; Sleeter & Grant, 2009), but rather are some broad and varied responses to the racial achievement gap. These teaching dispositions differ from specific multicultural approaches, because while it may be the case that most teachers agree that the achievement gap is not a desirable educational outcome, not all teachers are working from a particular multicultural perspective or approach to multicultural education. In some cases, teachers' dispositions in response to the racial achievement gap in schools are marked by a distinct inactivity. Thus, in the discussion that follows, I identify a range of common teacher responses to the racial achievement gap that differ from the various multicultural approaches that multicultural scholars have identified (Banks & McGee, 2013; Sleeter & Grant, 2009).

Due to the frequency to which I encounter these teaching dispositions myself, I couch the introduction to each teaching disposition in my own everyday subject positions as a teacher educator, mother of biracial, bilingual children, and as a multicultural education scholar. Throughout this discussion, it should become apparent that The Detached Teacher, The Deficit Thinker, and The Rugged Multicultural Teacher, much like the celebratory and contributions approaches to multicultural education, are problematic for the same reason: They fail to address the sociopolitical context of schooling. The first teaching disposition I introduce is: The Detached Teacher.

THE DETACHED TEACHER

The detached teacher has good intentions in mind and is not against the idea of educational equity by any means. In fact, the detached teacher wants all students to achieve, regardless of students' particular social positions and identities. For a variety of reasons, however, the detached teacher does not include educational transformation for social justice as part of their teaching agenda. In this section, I discuss two varieties of the detached teacher: Appeal to Numbers and A Case of Racist Teachers.

Appeal to Numbers

It's too bad that racial inequities still persist in schools. I'm sure that once racial minorities make up a bigger piece of the U.S. population, the problems with the achievement gap will be resolved. (Preservice Teacher)

As a race scholar in a teacher education program, I enthusiastically teach at least one multicultural education class—but often two or three—every semester. Among the many educational equity issues I have students examine in these classes, the racial achievement gap is of central importance. As students delve into the achievement gap data that characterizes almost every educational level and that appears across every achievement indicator, my pre-service teachers offer a plethora of responses that ultimately get them off the hook from taking on the task of transforming the school inequities they will inevitably face in their near futures as elementary and secondary teachers. The White preservice teacher referenced above, for example, provides an optimistic view on the achievement gap. This student believes that equity issues will get better when people of color are no longer the numerical minority. According to this common perception, the problem of the achievement gap is a matter of numbers, or more pointedly, a lack of numerical representation among students of color in U.S. schools. According to this perspective, the issue is simple: White students have had more access and equity in their schooling experiences because they represent the majority of students in U.S. schools. Said another way, U.S. schools simply cater to the student population who has the most prominent presence. In extension, once students of color have a stronger numerical presence, schools will do a better job at representing their voices, experiences, and histories, which will result in educational equity. By following this logic, teachers can figuratively "wash their hands" of the problem of the achievement gap, as it is believed that the achievement gap will take care of itself in time as demographics change.

The idea that the achievement gap will eventually disappear on its own, is indeed an optimistic position. As optimistic as this idea may be, however, it fails to consider the sociopolitical context of schooling. When we examine the sociopolitical context of schooling, we find that large-scale educational equity has yet to be achieved in U.S. schools—even in schools that have a majority minority population (Delpit, 2012; Gándara & Contreras, 2010). As an example, we can look at the vast land that makes up the state of Texas, where my teacher education program is located. In the state of Texas, Latinx[1] students alone make up 52 percent of the public school student population, outnumbering every other ethnic/racial population, including Whites, who represent 22 percent of the public school population (Texas Education

Agency, 2014). Further, the population of Latinx students combined with that of African American students in Texas makes up nearly 65 percent of the public school population (Texas Education Agency, 2014). Yet, even with these demographics, the achievement gap is as strong as it was 30 years ago, with Latinx and African American students being twice as likely to not finish high school as are White students, and with English Language Learners (ELLs) being the subgroup that drops out of high school most frequently (Intercultural Development Research Association, 2015).

The majority-minority phenomenon is not unique to Texas by any means. Currently, ethnic and racial minorities make up about half of the under 5 population in the U.S. and several states, including the District of Columbia, Hawaii, California, New Mexico, and Texas are already majority-minority states. Eight more states will be added to this list by 2020 (Kayne, 2013). It is also well documented that a resurgence in racial segregation over the last several decades in schools across the U. S. has resulted in an urban public school system that is almost entirely made up of African American, Latinx, and other students of color (Kozol, 2005; Orfield, 2008). Consistent with state and national data, the majority-minority demographics in urban school districts do not yield educational equity, but far too often, as Kozol (1991) blatantly articulates, *Savage Inequalities*. Scholars such as Darling-Hammond (2010) and Delpit (2012) elaborate on how students (largely African American and Latinx) in urban schools are the most underserved students in our public school system, receiving the least prepared and unskilled teachers, the least funding per student, a dumbed down curriculum, low expectations from teachers, and harsher disciplinary policies and punishments.

Not only does a stronger numerical representation in schools not guarantee school transformation or educational equity, a case can be made that Eurocentric and assimilationist agendas become even more cemented in schools that experience increased percentages of students of color. If we look to the state of Arizona, for example, racist and Eurocentric agendas have become increasingly explicit as the Latinx population continues to rise. Despite having a stronger Latinx presence in Arizona schools, the state has passed education laws that undermine Latinx-centric education and achievement, namely bans on bilingual education (Proposition 203) and ethnic studies programs (HB 2281) along with the racial profiling law (HB 1070). In the case of HB 2281, the ban on ethnic studies programs stemmed in Tucson, Arizona where 60 percent of the student population is Latinx. Interestingly enough, the Tucson Latinx students who were participating in the high school Mexican-American Studies (MAS) program were defying the achievement gap data in a variety of ways. For example, MAS students' high school graduation and college enrollment rates were higher than all other ethnic groups and they were outperforming all other ethnic and racial groups on Arizona's standardized achievement tests, including the Arizona Instrument for Measuring Standards (AIMS), which is the exit exam that is required for high school graduation (Ginwright & Cammarota, 2011). Despite this success, the MAS program, as well as all other ethnic studies programs in Arizona, have been dismantled. Ideologically speaking, the best-case scenario is that the academic achievement Latinx students experienced in the MAS program was considered irrelevant in the passing of this legislation, and at worst, it becomes the reason why Arizona schools have been mandated to restore the Eurocentric norm. As this example in Arizona illustrates, educational equity is anything but guaranteed in schools with high percentages of students of color. Even when great effort and grass-root leadership resulted in the establishment of a culturally responsive program that proved to be effective in diminishing the achievement gap, Latinx academic achievement is sabotaged. From what has happened in Arizona, it is important for educators to understand how racist ideologies, structures, and laws—the sociopolitical context of schooling—shape the educational landscape in ways that result in the miseducation of students of color, regardless of their numerical representation in schools.

When educators do not consider the sociopolitical dimensions of schooling, they may see optimism in a schooling context that has high numbers of students of color. They may assume that schools will naturally and inevitably transform as student demographics shift. From this disposition, the detached teacher exhibits a hands-off optimism toward educational equity issues. In this case, no action is necessary. Other "detached" teaching dispositions also garner inactivity, but are not characterized by the optimism that the "Appeal to Numbers" disposition espouses. The following discussion highlights a defeatist variation of the detached teacher: A Case of Racist Teachers.

A Case of Racist Teachers

At the school where I am placed for my student teaching, I have definitely come across some racist teachers and the things these teachers say are disgusting. The other day, I took my teacher mentor's class to the school track where they ran a mile and while we were there, there was this other teacher who took her class to the track. This teacher wanted her class to run faster, and she was yelling at this one Mexican girl in particular, telling her things like, "run like the cops are chasing you" and "run like your gangster friends want to kick your ass". It is these racist teachers who keep racism alive in schools. (White Student Teacher/Middle School)

A Case of Racist Teachers is a variation of the detached teacher, who in this case, holds racist teachers wholly responsible for the racial inequities we see in school practices and outcomes. The above quote from one of my White student teachers highlights her frustration with a racist teacher and points out that some teachers are simply racist and therefore are the culprits of the racial inequities we see in schools. When prompted, educators at all levels can often easily provide a variety of examples of the ways in which racist teachers communicate their racist beliefs/assumptions to their students, thereby creating racially hostile learning environments. Inferred from the multiple references my student teachers make about racist teachers and their offensive behaviors and attitudes, is that it is the racist teachers who are solely responsible for the racial disparities evidenced in student achievement outcomes.

While there certainly is truth and power in my student teachers' testimonials about racist teachers, I push them to expand their perceptions of how racism emanates in schools outside of the individual performances of racism they observe. Indeed, I push my student teachers to address the following question: Is it possible that these "bad apples" in our educational system are solely responsible for the ongoing and far-reaching nature of the achievement gap? No doubt, racist teachers create havoc in the lives of the students and families they come in contact with. Nevertheless, many multicultural and race scholars (Bonilla-Silva, 2014; Nieto, 2010, Nieto & Bode, 2012; Tatum, 2014) make clear that the problem of racial inequities is much more complex and inundated in our schools, than instances of individual racism. These critical multicultural scholars point to the much more impactful structural and institutional barriers as well as the ideological dimensions of schooling that are responsible for sustaining racial inequities on a massive scale. So no doubt individual racist teachers need to be held accountable for their actions, but we need to be cautious about any explanatory model that solely puts the onus of school achievement outcomes on teachers (Jones, 2015; Nieto & Bode, 2012; Tatum, 2014). While teachers certainly play a vital role in achieving educational equity, there are also broader structural challenges within the school system that even the best teacher cannot overcome (Milner, 2015).

Further, when we unpack the significance of the teaching disposition—A Case of Racist Teachers—we see that any resulting efforts to transform educational equity issues from this standpoint alone are likely futile. When we consider that the "racist" label only applies to some teachers, A Case of Racist Teachers ultimately gets most teachers off the hook from having to address racism in schools. As this teaching disposition has it, the only thing that can be done is to confront and transform those who are being identified as "racist teachers". Needless to say, this method of addressing racism in schools is riddled with problems. First, with the socially taboo nature of being labeled "racist," teachers are unlikely to self identify as "racist", much less be willing to attend professional development programs to address their racism. Given the social stigma of being considered racist, it is not surprising that among the thousands of students I have taught over the last two decades, not one of them has ever admitted to being a racist. Accordingly, when teachers detach themselves from the idea of being racist, they also detach themselves from the responsibility and work that needs to be done to confront racism. Seeing that the problem lies elsewhere, teachers may reason that it is the work of others—racist others—to deal with the problems of racism in schools. Bonilla-Silva (2014) identifies this phenomenon of the perpetual production of racial inequities with no self-identified racists, as "*Racism Without Racists*".

As I have stated, the two variations of the "detached teacher," Appeal to Numbers and A Case of Racist Teachers, have commonly surfaced in the multicultural education classes I teach in my teacher education program. These specific ways of responding to racial disparities in school achievement are by no means isolated to my classes though. The academic literature in the areas of multicultural education, teacher education, and whiteness studies regularly examines White students' and teachers' avoidance and disengagement with racial equity issues. The terminology that is used in these bodies of literature to identify White teachers' detachment from and disengagement in racial matters is vast: colorblindness (Bonilla-Silva, 2014; Bonilla-Silva & Dietrich, 2011; Howard, 2006; Nieto & Bode, 2012; Wise, 2010), white guilt (Nieto & Bode, 2012), white silence (LaDuke, 2009), white resistance (Dunn, Dotson, Ford, & Roberts, 2014), white fragility (DiAngelo, 2011) and white fatigue (Flynn, 2015), to name just a few. The concept of Whites avoiding racial issues is so often documented that Haviland (2008) has named White teachers' collective forms of resistance to race talk as "White educational discourse," defined as the "constellation of ways of speaking, interacting, and thinking in which White teachers gloss over issues of race, racism, and White supremacy in ways that reinforce the status quo, even when they have a stated desire to do the opposite" (p. 41).

The discussion in this section has focused on two variations of the detached teacher, which is characterized by a displacement of responsibility and overall inactivity in social justice issues that pertain to racism in schools. By no means do all White teachers uniformly disregard racial issues as will be seen in the upcoming sections. While the above examples are certainly some common responses to the educational inequities that occur along racial lines in schools, White teachers' understandings and ways of engaging in race issues are actually complex and can vary greatly. What is important to take away from this discussion though, is that one's understanding of how the racial achievement gap is produced, shapes his/her way of responding to it. In the case of the detached teacher, inactivity or a lack of teacher agency is a logical response to the racial achievement gap, because it is assumed that racism is either not part of the schooling experiences (appeal to numbers has it that curriculum and pedagogical approaches automatically adjust when a particular ethnic/racial linguistic group is prominently represented) or racial inequities is exclusively harnessed to individual teachers' distasteful ways of thinking about and interacting with students of color. As I explain in the upcoming sections, other ways of understanding the achievement gap can result in intervention as well as full-bodied notions of teacher advocacy. Up next is The Deficit Thinker.

THE DEFICIT THINKER

According to his test results, your son qualifies for our at-risk, pre-k program in the district. The test shows that his primary language is Spanish, which means that he is at-risk for school achievement. We believe that the extra year of schooling will provide him the opportunity to be successful in kindergarten and the later grades. (Pre-K Teacher)

Unfortunately, deficit thinking continues to hold explanatory power in understanding students' disparate schooling experiences and outcomes (Cammarota, 2011; Delpit, 2012; Valencia, 2011, 2015; Pimentel, 2011). Essentially, deficit thinking is a "blame the victim" (Valencia, 2011, p. 8) approach to understanding and addressing disparate achievement outcomes that occur along racial, economic, and linguistic lines. More specifically, deficit thinking blames students, their families, and communities for what is believed to be students' underachievement in school. As Valencia (2011) explains, "The deficit thinking model, at its core, is an endogenous theory—positing that the student who fails in school does so because of his/her internal deficits or deficiencies. Such deficits manifest, adherents allege, in limited intellectual abilities, linguistic shortcomings, lack of motivation to learn, and immoral behavior" (p. 8). Some teachers and other educators, who conceivably may be well intentioned, assume that students of color come to school with deficits that emanate from poverty, fluency in non-English languages, and/or deviations from Eurocentric cultural practices. Unlike the "racist" teacher I referenced in the previous section, the deficit thinker often means well and wants her/his students to achieve in school and in life. As such, deficit thinking teachers as well as the policies and programs that emanate from such thinking, aim to address the achievement gap by bridging the student and the school. Sleeter and Grant (2009) refer to this approach as Teaching the Exceptional and the Culturally Different, whereby specific policies, programs and practices aim to bridge the gap between students who are considered remedial and the current educational system.

Ruby Payne's, (2005) "culture of poverty" model for education is the epitome of such deficit thinking and reactive practices and programs. Payne's work primarily focuses on student deficits that perceivably result from poverty. Her framework offers 12 principles to help teachers effectively teach poor students (which often includes students of color). Many scholars (Cammarota, 2011; Delpit, 2012; Bomer, Edworin, May, & Semingson, 2008; Milner, 2015) have critiqued the inherent stereotypes and deficit thinking that Payne's program espouses. Nonetheless, her model for understanding poverty and schooling experiences are widely used in school districts with high percentages of poor students of color (Cammarota, 2011; Delpit, 2012).

Aside from Payne's model for education, there are many other ways educators attempt to address the so-called "deficits" students of color perceivably come to school with. In some cases, teachers "dumb down" the curriculum, so that learning is perceivably more manageable. Delpit (2012) explains that when teachers teach from a deficit perspective, they have a "tendency to teach less, to teach down, to teach for remediation" (p. 6). Whereas some teachers teach less, the strategy of other teachers and/or programs is to teach more, or more pointedly, for extended periods of time. In the case of teaching more, educators attempt to make up for students' supposed deficits by providing additional instruction, sometimes resulting in years of additional schooling. Programs such as Head Start and at-risk pre-k programs often target "at-risk" or "remedial" students who garner this deficit status because their cultural, linguistic, and/or economic identities have come to signify deficits or barriers to school achievement. The teaching disposition of the deficit thinker does not consider how students are positioned within a sociopolitical context that undermines the achievement of students of color and linguistic minorities. Rather, deficit thinking teachers take for granted that Eurocentric and monolingual English-language schooling experiences are politically neutral and even necessary for academic achievement. Thus, forms of intervention often take on seemingly "apolitical" policies, projects, and programs that attempt to make up for students' "deficits". Programs such as Head Start, at-risk pre-k programs, among many others attempt to address the achievement gap by providing "at-risk" students additional years of schooling with the hope that they can "catch up" and achieve at comparable levels with their White, English-speaking peers as a result of the additional schooling.

As is referenced in the quote at the beginning of this section, my son qualified to attend an at-risk pre-k program because he was a monolingual Spanish-speaker at the age of four-years-old. Within this deficit model of education, it did not matter that he already knew the pre-k curriculum before he started pre-k. Being a monolingual Spanish speaker was sufficient criteria for him to acquire the "at-risk" label on his academic records and additional schooling to make up for said deficits. I write extensively about my son's educational trajectory as an emerging bilingual student elsewhere (Pimentel, 2011).

In the spirit of exposing the racist function of deficit models of education, Alemán's (2013) documentary, *Stolen Education*, brings to light the educational policy of holding Latinx students back an additional two years in first grade in a South Texas school district to "make up" for Latinx students' so-called deficits. In this case, if the students made it all the way through high school (most did not), they would have attended 15 years of schooling and would graduate at 20–21 years old. More than anything, Alemán argues that this policy was used as a means to continue to segregate and provide an inferior education to Latinx students in a post-Brown schooling context. Alemán's work, as well as the many other critical educators who deconstruct deficit models of education, effectively document the educational hardships that result from deficit-oriented policies, programs, and practices. Overall, deficit thinking is a racist ideology that assumes that cultural and linguistic practices that differ from the White, middle-upper class, English-speaking norm, are somehow inferior and thereby serve as barriers, rather than resources, to learning. As Valencia and Solórzano (2004) so aptly put it, deficit thinking is a "destructive ideology" (p. 129) because it dumps educational failure on the laps of students and their parents all the while it "diverts attention" (p. 125) from and rationalizes the institutional factors that contribute to educational failure. Thus, by focusing on students' so-called deficits, the institutional and social aspects of schooling and school outcomes go unchecked and unaccounted for. Writing about the scapegoating nature of deficit thinking, Nieto (2017) explains that what is missing from the deficit thinking discourse is the "recognition of the institutional policies and practices—including vastly unequal resources, a Eurocentric curriculum, teachers who were poorly prepared to teach students of diverse backgrounds and, of course, racism and other biases—that made educational equity a natural outcome for large segments of the population" (p. 2). While deficit thinking differs from The Detached Teacher in that it is characterized by specific actions to address the achievement gap, these actions are misdirected. The Deficit Thinker focuses on assimilating the student to a school system that remains steadfast in being Eurocentric in focus. The next section focuses on the third teaching disposition: The Rugged Teacher—a teacher who actively tries to change how schools work.

THE RUGGED MULTICULTURAL TEACHER

[We need to] provide teacher candidates with opportunities to critique the system in ways that will help them choose a role as either agent of change or defender of the status quo. (Ladson-Billings, 2009, p. 133)

Whereas the detached teacher can be characterized by a lack of agency and the deficit thinker can be thought of as deferring agency to the student (as it is ultimately the student who must conform and/or assimilate to a Eurocentric school system in order to achieve), the rugged multicultural teacher is the epitome of teacher agency. Unlike the previously described teaching dispositions that fail to adequately address racial justice issues, my conception of the rugged multicultural teacher centers on the successes of teacher activism. There are a number of multicultural and race scholars who have narrated their own as well as other teachers' personal multicultural transformations and/or success at being culturally relevant teachers. Within these narratives, it is often the teacher's level of commitment, hard work, racial identity development, and/or critical consciousness that catapults teachers' practices to exemplar levels of multicultural teaching. These conceptions of teachers' work center on the notion of rugged individualism—that is—a teacher's ability to single-handedly transform her/himself, as well as student achievement outcomes, by aspiring to and embodying, albeit in individualized ways, specified teaching statuses and/or identities.

One version of the rugged multicultural teacher emerges in the multicultural and race literature that emphasizes the importance of Whites developing a positive racial identity (Carter, 1995; Helms, 1992; Howard, 2006). Howard (2006) specifically proposes a 3-stage model of White identity development that White teachers can use as a guide as they work toward transforming their White racial identities as well as their pedagogical and curricular practices. Howard's third, culminating stage—the "transformationist" stage—is the desired stage for White multicultural teachers who are committed to the task of dismantling White dominance. As a result of the personal racial identity transformation teachers undergo, and their willingness to commit to an ongoing learning experience in this final stage of White racial development, Howard affirms that teachers can deliver culturally responsive teaching. He states: "Transformative pedagogy is the place where our *passion for equity* intersects with our *cultural competence* and leads to *culturally responsive teaching* in our classrooms and schools [author's emphasis] (p. 133).

The concept of the rugged multicultural teacher also emerges in powerful, in-depth narratives of exemplar teachers who have developed a sense of critical

11

consciousness for social justice issues—a consciousness that often stems from a teacher's disadvantaged childhood upbringing or some sort of transformative event(s) that happened in a teacher's life in which s/he was exposed to and/or engaged in social justice issues (Cowey, 2006; Ladson-Billings, 2001, 2009; Michie, 2005, 2009; Milner, 2010; Nieto, 2010; Sleeter, 2015). These narratives of teachers' classroom practices provide the field of education, and teachers in particular, hope via role models who have achieved transformative pedagogies in their classrooms despite structural and institutional barriers. Indeed, success stories are a breath of fresh air in a field that often zooms in and examines the academic failures—not the academic successes—of students of color. Ladson-Billings (2009) makes this point when she states, "as the educational experiences of children of color are often characterized by despair, it is important to realize what educators of children of color are doing right, how they are "keeping the dream alive" (p. xvi).

There is no arguing that narratives on successful multicultural teachers provide invaluable influence to student teachers, teachers, and teacher educators who undertake similar goals themselves. However, in the larger arrangement of teaching dispositions, this is my concern: In so far as these narratives focus on the successes of accomplished multicultural teachers, therein lies an assumption that while some exceptional teachers succeed, many others fail at achieving multicultural practices in their classrooms. Thus, conceptualizations of the successful multicultural teacher can easily result in a dichotomy of multicultural achievement: success versus failure. Further, a teacher's occupancy on either side of the dichotomy becomes a direct reflection of her/his agency.

With this dichotomy in mind, I suggest that the very way many educators/ scholars discuss teachers' multicultural endeavors implicates a binary assessment of teachers' work and identities. While not necessarily the intention of multicultural and race scholars, I presume that the usage of the various terminology to name teachers' multicultural work/identities/statuses, at some level, is underpinned by the assumption that teachers can ultimately exemplify these romanticized notions of teaching. In the body of multicultural and antiracist literature, these highly esteemed teachers are variously referred to as being antiracist, nonracist, critical pedagogues, culturally relevant teachers, social justice teachers, allies, or multicultural teachers (Gay, 2010; Helms, 1992; Howard, 2006; Ladson-Billings, 2009; Lawrence & Tatum, 1997; Sleeter, 1992).

From these honorable models of critical multicultural teaching, teachers' everyday multicultural practices are likely assessed by using either/or logic (e.g., multicultural/ not multicultural, racist/anti-racist, culturally relevant/not culturally relevant). This binary logic is embedded in many educational mottos I have come across that essentially say: "If you are not changing the problem, you are part of the problem". Consistent with this reasoning, Ladson-Billings (2009) points out the pivotal role teacher educators play in assisting student teachers to consciously choose what kind of educator they want to be. Ladson-Billings' quote at the beginning of this section is relevant here: "[We need to] provide teacher candidates with opportunities to critique the system in ways that will help them choose a role as either agent of change or defender of the status quo" (p. 133). As a critical educator myself, I appreciate Ladson-Billing's encouraging push for teachers to actively challenge the racial status quo in schools. My concern with such binary logic, however, is that the multicultural work of many teachers is not represented on either side of this binary. What is missing are the various teachers who are committed to social justice issues and strive to be effective multicultural teachers, yet in many ways and for a variety of reasons, feel unsuccessful at fulfilling such a vision. These are the teachers I feature in the case study chapters in this book. Thus, this book seeks not to examine the extremities of teacher agency (complacency versus rugged activism), but similar to Urrieta's (2009) work on Chicano/a activism: "I am interested in the space of practice (activism) in between the two axes" (p. 154). Urrieta, elaborating on the concept of activism, explains that, "Active participation is not just about reactive practice, or resistance practice, nor is it about reproductive practices. The focus should be on what happens in between this dichotomy" (p. 159).

In my examination of the various renditions of the rugged multicultural teacher in multicultural education literature, I conclude that the concept of the rugged multicultural teacher does not adequately capture the pedagogical constraints that emerge in the particular sociopolitical contexts teachers encounter in their classrooms and schools. With this being said, it is my position that narratives of the rugged multicultural teacher, much like the teaching dispositions of the detached teacher and the deficit thinker, do not adequately consider the sociopolitical context in which teachers and students are embedded. As Strom and Martin (2017) make clear, there are clear limitations to singling out teachers as the sole change factor in the classroom: "By filtering out all elements except the teacher and assigning a causal relation between the teacher and learning, this perspective of teaching positions the teacher as an autonomous actor, students as passive, and contexts as neutral" (p. xii). Simply put, the notion of the rugged multicultural teacher overly relies on a teacher's agency to overcome any obstacles he/she may encounter in her/his work as a multicultural educator. The overreliance on teachers' personal will and effort is the same critique that neoliberals encounter when they unproblematically assume that students of color can overcome educational equity issues and achieve academically by simply having the motivation and a strong work ethic—essentially a pull yourself up by your own bootstraps argument (Villanueva, 1993). The bootstrap argument overly relies on the concepts of individual effort and merit, just as the concept of the rugged multicultural teacher overly relies on the concept of teacher agency. Both of these conceptions of agency are largely stripped from the sociopolitical and sociohistorical landscape of U.S. society and schooling, which has a long history of racial exploitation that continues to impact our personal and social lives in both subtle and explicit ways. The legacy of racism, I argue, cannot be overcome solely through robust conceptions of teacher agency. Thus, the purpose of this book is to move beyond both bankrupt and rugged notions of teacher advocacy by examining instead both the possibilities and impossibilities—the (im)possibilities—of multicultural education. As such, my particular framing of teachers' multicultural practices seeks to avoid binary conceptions of multiculturalism, which result in understanding teachers' multicultural endeavors in terms of success or failure. As will be seen in the case-study chapters of this book, I theorize teachers' multicultural practices in contradictions—teacher practices that both reinforce and challenge the racial status quo.

THE (IM)POSSIBLE MULTICULTURAL TEACHER

> I don't believe I am a good multicultural teacher. Perhaps you should look at some other teachers for your study. (Mr. Potts/4th & 5th-Grade Teacher)

So far in this chapter, I have alluded to the idea of coherent teaching dispositions: The Detached Teacher, The Deficit Thinker, and the Rugged Teacher. It may be inferred from this discussion on teaching dispositions that teachers can holistically exemplify these conceptions of teaching. Yet my principle argument in this book is that teachers' pedagogical practices cannot be understood as existing outside the inequitable power relations that define the sociopolitical context of teaching. From this viewpoint, I assert that teachers' multicultural practices, even when they put forth their best efforts, are necessarily conflicted and incoherent, rather than static assemblages of pure pedagogical practices.

My take on teacher agency varies greatly from the previously described "coherent" teaching dispositions. Unlike the lack of agency that represents the detached teacher, the misguided agency that typifies the deficit thinker, and the hyper-agency that represents the rugged multicultural teacher, my conception of teacher agency is one that is diffused. Drawing from Strom & Martin's (2017) concept of "becoming teacher" (p. 8), it is my position that teachers cannot reach static notions of multiculturalism or antiracism. Rather, teachers' work must be understood in terms of their involvement in uncharted and ongoing multicultural projects that are situated in schooling contexts, that for the most part, work against the goals of multicultural education. As a result, teachers' multicultural practices are messy and often incoherent. In the case-study chapters, it should become evident that my goal is not to evaluate whether a participating teacher has reached a certain level of multicultural status, racial identity, actualized a coherent teaching orientation, or even whether he/she has succeeded or failed in their multicultural endeavors. Rather, my goal is to examine the (im)possibilities of multicultural education that emanate from the pedagogical practices of hard working, committed, critical-minded, and knowledgeable White teachers who try to work against the grain of the racial status quo.

As I move forward to theorize the (im)possible multicultural teacher, I want to make clear that by no means do I think teacher agency is null in the social justice work teachers do. Teacher agency is indeed an important piece to teacher advocacy and should not be underestimated. However, when we consider the sociopolitical context in which teachers work, we come to see how teachers' multicultural practices become constrained and conflicted. We must understand that teachers are not free-wielding agents who can carve out idealistic practices and outcomes in a less than ideal world. Teachers do not teach in a vacuum, and as Milner (2015) states, teachers "must be prepared to negotiate, balance, and combat pervasive counterproductive discourses and practices that already exist and that might work against reform" (p. 65). On a similar note, Tatum (2014) claims that people, including teachers of all races, can never fully remove themselves from the smog of racism that saturates our society. We are constantly breathing in the "smog of racism" and it is affecting us, whether we realize it or not. Nieto and Bode (2012) further assert that teachers "are the products of educational systems that have a history of racism, exclusion, and debilitating pedagogy. As a consequence, their practices may reflect their experiences, and they may unwittingly perpetuate policies and approaches that are harmful to many of their students" (p. 7).

As I examine the participating teachers' multicultural work, I draw from process-oriented approaches to multicultural education (Nieto & Bode, 2012; Banks & McGee, 2013). Process-oriented approaches to multicultural education suggest that becoming a multicultural education teacher is an ongoing endeavor—always in process but never quite achieved. Nieto and Bode (2012) state, "…Multicultural education is, above all, a process. It is ongoing and dynamic because no one ever stops becoming a multicultural person and knowledge is never complete" (p. 53). Similarly, Banks and McGee (2013) argue, "Multicultural education is… a process whose goals will never be fully realized" (p. 4) and "Multicultural education is a continuing process because the idealized goals it tries to actualize—such as educational equality and the eradication of all forms of discrimination—can never be fully achieved in human society" (p. 21). From these viewpoints, it is assumed that teachers never fully reach or personify a multicultural ideal—and further—social justice work and the transformative process is never complete.

In my conception of the (im)possible multicultural teacher, I diverge from concepts that can be considered "coherent" or "pure" pedagogies. In my examination of the participating teachers' pedagogical practices, I draw from concepts such as "hybrid pedagogy" (Buendía, 2000) and "borderland pedagogy" (Buendía, Gitlin, & Doumbia, 2003)—terms that refer to the fusion of competing ideologies in teachers' pedagogical practices, which can include, for example, elements of the deficit thinker and the rugged multicultural teacher. My approach to understanding the teachers' multicultural practices in the case studies included in this book also parallel Britzman's (2003) conception of teacher advocacy. According to Britzman, teaching practices, no matter how idealized they may be imagined in teacher education programs, cannot be realized in the actual teaching contexts teachers are placed in. In her examination of student teachers, Jamie Owl and Jack August, Britzman reveals the complexity of teaching that is infused with both promise and peril. As Britzman makes clear in her work, pedagogical perfection can never be achieved. Specifically in the profession of teaching, the idiom, practice makes perfect, does not apply. Rather, as the title of her book proclaims, *Practice Makes Practice*. This could not

15

be more true for the teachers featured in this book. Despite their best multicultural efforts, they never reach perfection, yet they all are determined to keep teaching from a critical perspective, with the hope that they will make small transformative changes. Before I move on to the case study chapters, I briefly introduce each of the teachers who participated in this study: Mr. Potts, Ms. DeGraw, and Megan.

MR. POTTS

Mr. Potts is a 35-year-old White man, who is married to a blind woman and has three young children. He has been teaching elementary school for 10 years in various models of bilingual education, including Transitional (Early-Exit) Bilingual, Two-Way Dual Language, and One-Way Dual Language programs. When Mr. Potts was nine years old, his family moved to Chile, where he became fluent in Spanish. In Chile, Mr. Potts occupied the identities of language and ethnic-minority, and went through an experience whereby the knowledge he held, and which could only be expressed in English, was rendered non-existent in a school system that operated solely in Spanish. After an initial academic assessment, Mr. Potts was placed in a grade level below what he had already completed in the U.S., and he was demoralized in a number of other ways, such as through the changing of his name. As a result of Mr. Potts' experiences as a child, he became attuned to the ways in which language politics can work to disengage and cut off students' opportunities for school success. He knew that language minority students in the United States often experience what he experienced as a child in Chile: the systematic invalidation of students' knowledge and worth. Reflecting Mr. Potts' critical awareness and knowledge of language politics in educational settings, his pedagogical practices center on advocating for his Latinx, Spanish-speaking students. Mr. Potts teaches a fourth- and fifth-grade, stand-alone, two-way dual language bilingual class in English and Spanish at Viewpoint Elementary.

MS. DEGRAW

Ms. DeGraw is a 45-year-old White woman who is lesbian, has a partner, and is the mother of two children. Her son is 14 years old and her daughter is 12 years old. Ms. DeGraw is Italian-American and grew up Catholic. When Ms. DeGraw was 25 years old, she obtained a bachelor's degree in French. At this time, she met her husband-to-be and married him three years later. Their marriage lasted for 9 years, during which time she had her two children, worked at a wine store, and started a small business, where she baked cookies and sold them to local coffee shops. Later in life, at the age of 37-years-old, Ms. DeGraw went through a number of significant life changes. At this point in her life, she divorced her husband, sold her business, went back to school to obtain a bachelor's degree in education as well as a teaching certificate, and came out as a lesbian. Ms. DeGraw is in her second year of teaching at Drew Middle School—the magnet ESL middle school for the school district. She teaches seventh- and eighth-grade ESL classes and an elective video recording class.

MEGAN

Megan is a 26-year-old White, upper-class woman, who has been married for 4 years and has no children. Megan describes herself as an over-achiever. For example, when she was in high school, she took so many Advanced Placement (AP) classes that she only had 2 years of college remaining after she graduated from high school. She received her college degree in English and then went to France to live for a year, where she obtained an additional degree in French literature. When she returned from France, she enrolled in a teacher certification program and obtained her teaching certification one year later. She received her first teaching position three years ago at Esplanade—the alternative high school in the district. The classes Megan teaches at Esplanade include: Math, AP English, Dance, School Success, and Advisory.

Megan was raised in and continues to live a very privileged lifestyle with a high socioeconomic status. Her father is the owner of several successful businesses and is independently wealthy. As a result of Megan's financial wealth, she has always lived in the wealthiest, gated communities of the city. Even until this day, Megan's father supports her and her husband financially to the extent that her paychecks from her teaching position go untouched and directly into a savings account. As can be imagined, Megan's life and schooling experiences have been isolated among all wealthy, White people. The only poor people and people of color that Megan came into contact with as she was growing up were the Mexican men who came to do her family's yard work.

Because Megan has had minimal experiences with oppression, as well as little to no contact with racial and/or linguistic others as she was growing up, working at Esplanade has provided her with some of her first encounters with racial/linguistic/economic diversity and oppression. Unlike Mr. Potts and Ms. DeGraw, who had first-hand life experiences with oppression, Megan is learning for the first time about social injustices in regard to race, language, and socio-economic status.

NOTE

[1]   I intentionally use the word Latinx as a gender-neutral term instead of Latino and Latina, which are gender-specific terms.

MR. POTTS' DUAL LANGUAGE CLASSROOM

The school bell rings promptly at 10:35am at which point all of Mr. Potts' fourth- and fifth-grade students, except Javier, rush outside in the 40 degree weather to play hand-ball, four-square, freeze tag, and soccer. Javier, with a concerned look on his face, immediately approaches Mr. Potts: "Señor Potts, perdí uno de mis guantes. ¿Me puede ayudar Ud. a encontrarlo? Mr. Potts: Sí mi'jo, vamos afuera para mirar si está en el suelo (Javier: Mr. Potts, I lost one of my gloves. Can you help me find it? Mr. Potts: Yes my son, let's go outside and see if it is on the ground).

Mr. Potts' classroom is one of only two classrooms at Viewpoint Elementary where Latinx students are encouraged to speak their native language, Spanish. Even though there is not a bilingual program at Viewpoint Elementary, Mr. Potts, along with a teacher in kindergarten, have decided to model their classrooms after the highly esteemed Two-Way Dual Language bilingual program (referred to as dual language hereafter). The dual language model is an integrated program where roughly half the students are native English speakers and the other half of students are native speakers of another language (In Mr. Potts' class, roughly half his students are native Spanish speakers). The overarching goals of dual language programs are for students to become bilingual and biliterate and experience high levels of academic achievement as they learn core content through instruction in both languages (For more on dual language programs, see: Freeman, Freeman, & Mercuri, 2004; Hamayan, Genesee, & Cloud, 2013; Lindholm-Leary, 2001).

According to multicultural scholars—and clearly the guiding multicultural principle in Mr. Potts' class—native language instruction is an essential component to multicultural education. Mr. Potts has implemented native language instruction in his class by adapting the dual language model, because as he explains, "It is the only program that positions Latinx, Spanish-speaking students favorably in a school setting". He further explains that the perception of Latinx students' "educability" within a school setting greatly depends upon the bilingual program they participate in.

> Mr. Potts: I've taught bilingual education my entire teaching career and whenever Hispanics are bunched up into one program, it is looked at by the school as the 'special' program. They still think of those kids that go into a class all day, where they're separated, as the kids that can't handle it, a normal classroom. It's always in a certain part of the building and the English-speaking kids and teachers don't know anything about it except that

the Spanish-speaking kids go there to get help. But when they're in a dual language immersion class with English speaking kids, then it's, 'Oh-that's the gifted class where everyone is learning a second language'. As soon as English speakers are learning a second language, it's a gifted program.

I first heard about Mr. Potts and what he was doing in his classroom from one of my friends who had two children attending Viewpoint Elementary. A critical Latinx educator herself, she appreciated that Mr. Potts was working against the grain of the school, and the state for that matter, by advocating for Latinx school achievement by teaching school content in Spanish. Based on her recommendation, as well as what I had heard from other teachers, I set up a meeting with Mr. Potts in his classroom after school one day. During this meeting I began to explain to Mr. Potts that my friend was impressed with what he was doing in his classroom and that she considered him a strong advocate for Latinx students attending Viewpoint Elementary. I further explained that I thought he would be perfect for my research study, which was focusing on successful multicultural teachers.

Before I had time to say much more about my study, Mr. Potts was paged on the school intercom, requesting that he come to the main office to translate for a Spanish-speaking parent. Mr. Potts excused himself from our meeting and left me alone in his classroom. He was not gone for more than five minutes, but that provided me an opportunity to observe the physical environment of Mr. Potts' classroom. What was most obvious was that his class was located outside of and in the back of the main school building in a portable trailer. I thought to myself, "This is typical of bilingual classrooms—physically and conceptually marginalized from the larger school!". All the windows in the trailer were covered in sun-faded sheets of construction paper that were being used to block out the bright sunrays. As I looked around the inside of Mr. Potts' classroom, I noted a distinct disorder and messiness to the room. Several word charts were falling off the walls. There were large piles of papers and books scattered about the room and a big cardboard box (originally used to store paper towels) on the floor next to his desk. This is where he stored ungraded student assignments and the box was over half full! The floor was sprinkled with a considerable amount of popcorn, pieces of broken pencils, candy wrappers, and other little pieces of paper.

When Mr. Potts returned from the main office, he sat with me at the students' tables where he proceeded to forthrightly tell me that he appreciated the complement about his teaching but he did not think that he was a good teacher. He went on to say:

Mr. Potts: I used to be a good teacher, but I'm not a good teacher anymore.
Charise: Why do you say that?
Mr. Potts: I just don't have the support from the school here and I don't get the supplies like I used to at the school I was at before.

He then pointed to a shelf of *Harry Potter* books (a set in Spanish and English) his students were currently reading and explained how difficult it was for him to order the Spanish versions of the book or any other Spanish materials for that matter. He continued to explain, "I basically have to translate all the English materials into Spanish and deliver all instruction in Spanish and English, which is a tremendous amount of work and unheard of in a true dual language program". He went on, humbly describing his class as chaotic, loud, and messy. He even told me that if I wanted to see some good examples of teaching, that I ought to visit some other teachers at Viewpoint Elementary, and then proceeded to provide me names. I assured him that I wanted to learn more about his classroom and his struggle to implement multicultural practices, so he tentatively agreed that I could sit in his class during the school day. From my class observations that followed this initial meeting, I was impressed with what I saw unfold in his classroom, so I was delighted when he later enthusiastically agreed to participate in my research study.

In this chapter I provide a detailed analysis of Mr. Potts' (im)possible multicultural practices. Within this analysis, I show that despite Mr. Potts' modest assessment of his teaching, there were many times when he was able to successfully advocate for his Latinx students through his adaptation of the dual language program in his classroom. However, the idea of the unwavering multicultural teacher, or what I have termed the "rugged multicultural teacher", did not capture his teaching experiences. Consistent with his own self-appraisal, and with my conception of the (im)possible multicultural teacher, there were many aspects of Mr. Potts' classroom and teaching that worked against his multicultural goals and instead supported the racial order of the school and social contexts in which he worked. Important to this analysis then, is the complexity of his multicultural practices. While he no doubt advocated for Latinx student achievement, his "multicultural practices" were not able to safeguard his classroom, his own pedagogical practices included, from the production of inequitable schooling.

As I move forward in developing Mr. Potts' case study, I argue, as I have elsewhere (Pimentel, 2011), that students' language serves as a proxy for race. That is, within the sociopolitical context in which Mr. Potts teaches, students' language(s) are racialized via specific language ideologies. Language ideologies are defined as "networks or beliefs about language that position human subjects within a social order" (Shuck, 2006, p. 259). At Viewpoint Elementary, I have identified three specific language ideologies: (1) language deficit, (2) English first, and (3) White superiority. These specific ideologies guide all students' schooling experiences at Viewpoint Elementary by advancing the following assumptions: (1) non-English languages are not academic languages, (2) the business of learning at school cannot be fully achieved until students are fluent in the English language, and (3) White, English-dominant students' educational experiences and achievement must take precedence over all others. Before I delve into the complexity of Mr. Potts' multicultural practices, I first introduce Viewpoint Elementary as well as describe the sociopolitical context in which the school is situated.

VIEWPOINT ELEMENTARY

I collected ethnographic research data from Mr. Potts' fourth- and fifth-grade classroom at Viewpoint Elementary (For a full description of methodology, see the appendix of this book). Viewpoint Elementary has 720 students, 73% of who qualify for free or reduced-cost lunches and nearly 60% of the student body are students of color and learning English as their second language. The Latinx student population consists of 53 percent of the student body at Viewpoint Elementary. Viewpoint Elementary is one of many elementary and middle schools within the school district where White, English monolingual students are the minority. Despite the large numbers of students of color, low SES, and ELLs attending Viewpoint Elementary, 94 percent of the teachers at Viewpoint Elementary are White, middle-class, and monolingual English speakers.

Sociopolitical Context

The sociopolitical context at Viewpoint Elementary is not much different from elementary schools across the nation. U.S. schools, for the most part, do not provide adequate language programs for their English Language Learners (ELLs). The National Education Association (2005) states that, "Only 8 percent of ELLs receive extensive instruction designed specifically to meet their learning needs—including 10 or more hours of ESL instruction per week, content instruction that is specifically modified for ELLs and at least 25 percent use of the students' native language for instructional purposes" (http://www.nea.org/home/13598.htm). Further, the state in which Viewpoint Elementary is located passed 'Official English' legislation, resulting in all official government business (e.g. public documents, records legislation, regulations, hearings, official ceremonies, and public meetings) having to be conducted in English only. While this legislation does not directly impact public schools, the indirect sentiment of the law is that everything in schools should be conducted in English. Not surprising, there were only a handful of schools in the entire state that were implementing a bilingual program.

Consistent with the overall state and national sentiments on bilingual education, Viewpoint Elementary as a whole did not value minority languages, and as a result, was not home to a bilingual education program—a program that would provide students the opportunity to move through each grade with a continuous focus on developing literacy and core content in English and Spanish. ELLs who were not enrolled in one of the Spanish-speaker spots in either Mr. Potts' or Ms. Percy's (a kindergarten teacher) classes, were mainstreamed into English-instructed classrooms.

District

As I continue to define the sociopolitical context of Viewpoint Elementary, I share several examples of how language ideologies surfaced in school activities and decision-making processes. The first language ideology—language deficit ideology—assumes that non-English languages are low-class, non-academic languages, and as such, fluency in a non-English language is treated as a condition that must be overcome. Mr. Potts was well aware of this language ideology and explained to me that it often popped up, even in his interactions with the school district. For example, when Mr. Potts attended a district meeting where administrators were discussing various risk factors that were impacting students' academic achievement, they employed the language deficit ideology. Mr. Potts explains:

> Mr. Potts:　During this meeting, one of the district administrators held up a poster board with a road map on it and they were identifying all these different pot holes or barriers students face in their education and one of the pot holes they pointed to on the map was students who speak a second language.

The district administrators also discussed a number of strategies teachers could use to help students overcome their language barrier, and in the process, not only gain English fluency, but perceivably academic success.

Viewpoint Elementary Teachers

The language deficit ideology also surfaced in Mr. Potts' interactions with Viewpoint Elementary teachers. Echoing the district administrators' perspectives on language minority students, many teachers at Viewpoint Elementary similarly argued that language minority students were at a disadvantage, and for this reason, they could not see any benefits students gained from being enrolled in Mr. Potts' classroom. These teachers reasoned that instruction in Spanish was time away from English instruction, which is what language minority students, they argued, desperately needed. Many teachers at Viewpoint Elementary were straight-forward in telling Mr. Potts that they thought his class was a "waste of time", and not only for Latinx students, but perhaps even more so for the White, English-dominant students who struggled in English Language Arts (ELA). Teachers' primary concerns centered on how White students were performing in Mr. Potts' class and how his class may impede upon their academic development (especially in ELA), which brought to light the white superiority ideology. Mr. Potts expresses White teachers' primary concern about his class:

> Mr. Potts:　If it's a [White] child that's below grade level [in ELA] then they're, then that's what they have big concerns about, because they've gone, they need to learn to read and write in English. And if they can't do that in English, why are we wasting their educational time on another language. And yeah, that's been a big thing.

Many teachers, as Mr. Potts points out, have a problem with his class because it perceivably prohibits or prolongs students', and especially White students' process

23

of achieving what is perceived to be the prerequisite to learning: English fluency and literacy. As such, this example also illuminates the second language ideology: English first.

Dual Language up for a Vote

Based on how Viewpoint Elementary teachers assess the importance of Mr. Potts' dual language class, it is not surprising that when faced with the opportunity to implement a school-wide dual-language program, teachers overwhelmingly voted not to implement the program. As I was collecting data in Mr. Potts' stand-alone dual language class, the Educational Equity Officer from the school district had secured a one-million dollar grant to pilot five dual language programs in elementary schools across the school district. Viewpoint Elementary was one of the schools that were considering whether or not to become part of the grant and implement a school-wide dual language program. Over the course of several months leading up to the vote on whether or not to implement a dual language program, staff meetings were used as a time and place when teachers were to become informed about the research on bilingual education and the different types of bilingual programs. As part of this learning process, teachers received readings, attended special sessions with experts on bilingual education, and participated in question and answer sessions. With the vote just a few short months away, the topic of bilingual education became a reoccurring theme on staff meeting agendas—a hand out that was passed out at the beginning of each staff meeting.

As I observed the proceedings of these staff meetings, I found that the staff meetings provided a window into teachers' thoughts on bilingual education. In one staff meeting in particular, while a teacher was waiting for the meeting to get started, he read over the agenda. When he came across the topic of bilingual education as one of the bulleted items that once again would be discussed in the meeting, he threw the paper up in the air and responded out loud for others to hear:

Teacher: Not this shit again!

At another staff meeting, teachers were engaged in a discussion on bilingual education and teachers started to voice their concerns, to which Mr. Potts often responded. One teacher was concerned about the school's transitory problem and how that would potentially affect the implementation of the dual language program. Mr. Potts responded to this teacher's concern by addressing all the teachers in the meeting, telling them they needed to stop using excuses and implement the program.

Mr. Potts: We cannot use that as an excuse, because it will always be an issue, and if it was an issue that affected whether students need language development then it wouldn't make any sense to introduce language programs at the middle-school level either. It is crucial that they have a bilingual program in the early age, because right now students aren't learning how to read in their first language, which has a large effect on their English literacy.

As the meeting continued, another teacher voiced her concern about students with learning disabilities.

Teacher: How can we expect these [special education] students to participate in this program? They already struggle to learn as it is, and now we expect them to learn in another language?

Mr. Potts: We would have support to help these kids. To be honest, I am taken aback at the contradictions here. We have always expected our Spanish-speaking students with learning disabilities to learn English, no questions asked. But now if it's an English-speaking student learning Spanish, there is all of this concern.

Noting both the hostility and ongoing concerns teachers had about bilingual education, I asked Mr. Potts in an interview if he could explain why teachers did not embrace the idea of bilingual education. In this interview, I discovered that the teachers' concerns were not solely based on the educational experiences of students, but were primarily about the teachers themselves.

Mr. Potts: They're not necessarily against a traditional bilingual program [a program that would contain all Spanish-dominant students]. It [traditional bilingual program] saves the teachers. It's like "oh OK, they're [Spanish-dominant students] a brand new arrival and we don't have to deal with them. They can go to your class instead [a bilingual class]." For example, it started impacting them when Ms. Percy [kindergarten teacher] implemented a dual language class in the lower grades and started taking English kids into this environment. That caused a lot of concern. She was taking English-speaking kids out of their classes and replacing them with Spanish-speaking kids. So Spanish-speaking kids are the problem for these teachers. They don't want them in their classrooms. With the traditional bilingual classes, they're OK with that because it's like "well good, somebody else deals with the problem".

Feeding into the language deficit ideology, these teachers did not want "deficient" students in their classes. According to Mr. Potts, a traditional bilingual program is preferred, and teachers would likely vote to implement this program, because it is seen as a remedial program that can contain and "deal with" all the "remedial" [read Latinx] students. In essence, a traditional bilingual program would get White, English monolingual teachers off the hook from having to educate what they consider "remedial" students. In extension, the dual language program—an integrated bilingual approach—is not an attractive option because, as the district has proposed it, this program would leave Latinx [read remedial] students in White,

English monolingual teachers' classes for the portion of their instruction that would be in English. Evidently, these "remedial" students take the spots of potentially superior White, English-speaking children.

To complicate matters further, teachers disapprove of the dual language program because it potentially jeopardizes their job security. From what has been proposed, the dual language program would require Viewpoint Elementary to hire more bilingual teachers, which would mean that three English-monolingual teachers would have to relocate to another elementary school. In addition to this, English monolingual teachers would not be able to use their seniority at the school to safeguard their teaching positions. Mr. Potts explains:

Mr. Potts: If they pass the dual language program, they will need to get a rid of three English-speaking teachers, because they will need seven English- and seven Spanish-speaking teachers for the program and they only have four Spanish-speaking teachers right now. It would also mean that those with seniority as far as time teaching will not have priority over those Spanish-speaking teachers who have only been here for 1 to 2 years. So it would be possible that a bilingual teacher with only one year of experience at Viewpoint Elementary would keep her job, while a teacher with 12 years of experience would lose hers.

In the end, the teaching staff at Viewpoint Elementary, by and large, voted against implementing a dual language program in order to secure their teaching positions as well as to advocate for segregated classrooms. Informed by the language deficit ideology that frames language minority students as undesirable students, as well as teachers' concern over the stability of their own teaching positions (White superiority), it became clear that teachers were more interested in securing their White privilege instead of considering what would be best for the educational achievement of the students at Viewpoint Elementary.

MR. POTTS' DUAL LANGUAGE CLASSROOM

In explaining the sociopolitical context in which Viewpoint Elementary is situated, I have identified a number of ways in which language ideologies impact how the school district and teaching staff think about both the White and Latinx students who attend Viewpoint Elementary. In what follows, I examine how these language ideologies impact Mr. Potts' classroom. I begin this discussion by focusing on who is enrolled in Mr. Potts' classroom and how these decisions are made.

Placement Strategies

There are 12 White, native English speakers and 13 Latinx, native Spanish speakers in Mr. Potts' class. He teaches a combination fourth- and fifth-grade class so that fourth-grade students have the option to take his bilingual class an additional year in fifth grade. Most fifth graders were enrolled in Mr. Potts' class in the fourth grade. In designing his makeshift dual language classroom, Mr. Potts made it clear to the teaching staff and administration at Viewpoint Elementary that he wanted an ethnic/racial and linguistic mix of students in his classroom. Beyond this request, he had no say in terms of who ended up in his classroom. Decisions about who was placed in Mr. Potts' classroom was entirely determined by teacher referral and White, English-monolingual parents who wanted their children to benefit from dual language instruction. As I demonstrate in this section, the selection process of who participated in Mr. Potts' class greatly impacted Mr. Potts' attempts to advocate for Latinx educational achievement through his adaptation of the dual language model.

In deciding who would be placed in Mr. Potts' classroom, teachers' decisions were often guided by the language deficit and English first ideologies. As explained previously in this chapter, the English first ideology has it that English fluency is a prerequisite to all learning. As such, teaching Spanish is deemed (1) an interruption to students' development in English language fluency/literacy and (2) an extracurricular enrichment activity for students who have proved their mastery in English fluency/literacy. In keeping with this logic, teachers are very strategic as to whom they refer to Mr. Potts' classroom. To begin, teachers refer their highest-level White, English-dominant students to Mr. Potts' class. Teachers reason that the class is a gifted situation for these students, because they have already met the prerequisite of English fluency by being at or above grade level in English literacy and thus can perceivably handle the academic rigor of learning a second language without jeopardizing their English language fluency/literacy.

Unlike the White, English-dominant students who enroll in Mr. Potts' class so they can take advantage of an academically enriched learning program, the Latinx, Spanish-dominant students are placed in Mr. Potts' class as a last resort effort to address their "behavioral" or "academic" problems. Teachers believe that the low-achieving Latinx students are better placed in Mr. Potts' class because of his ability to deliver core content in a language they can understand. Thus, the goal of placing Latinx, Spanish-dominant students in Mr. Potts' class is not to participate in a linguistically enriched class where they can further build upon the linguistic skills they have already developed in their native language in addition to English language development, but rather intervention to a process whereby students fall further and further behind in core curriculum due to the inaccessibility of instruction in their native language. An added benefit of this placement strategy for White, English monolingual teachers is that this placement strategy takes the most "troubled" (behaviorally or academically) Latinx students out of White teachers' classrooms so they do not have to deal with the "problem" students themselves. The other, "more teachable" Latinx students, who are well on their way to learning English, stay in mainstream, English-instructed classrooms so they can continue to develop their English fluency/literacy and have a real chance at being "educated".

In sum, the goals of the strategic placement of students in Mr. Potts' class are: (1) so that high achieving White students who have perceivably already mastered the English language can enhance their educational experience by learning a second language, and (2) so that "deficient" Latinx students do not become hopelessly behind in curriculum. In an interview, Mr. Potts talks at length about the placement strategies that are used in his class.

Mr. Potts: Um, when they pick the kids that come into my class, because it hasn't been a dual-language program since kindergarten, I get the lowest fourth graders that are Hispanic. It matters not that they've been here all the way from kindergarten and another student arrived a week before. They'll [teachers] be "oh but this child [new arrival] does so well. And they can function in the [mainstream] classroom. This child ["remedial"] needs your help". But it's like "but no, this is supposed to be set up to help them with language," you know. "But no, no, no. This child is doing fine. This child is never going to read unless they're in your class". So I get like um, Fernando and Miguel and Mario who have been in the United States their whole education and don't know their alphabet in either language and that's not really what the program is set up for. So English-speaking kids in my class with the dual language are seen as being gifted and bright. Uh, Spanish-speaking kids are getting that reputation amongst the parents that come in and see both, but teachers still see my class for Hispanic students, as a class for students with special needs.

While these placement strategies arguably meet the needs of White, English-monolingual teachers, Mr. Potts explains that there are many undesirable outcomes to this process. One of the major outcomes, as Mr. Potts points out, is a clear discrepancy in reading levels and general academic competencies between the White, English-dominant students and the Latinx, Spanish-dominant students. Thus, despite Mr. Potts' attempt at implementing a dual language model in his classroom in an effort to position Latinx students as equally knowledgeable and resourceful as their White, English-speaking peers, the placement strategies create a situation where Latinx students are considered remedial learners, much the same way they are in mainstream, English-instructed classrooms. In an interview, Mr. Potts discusses the challenge of teaching his "uneven" class and how, despite his intentions, he feels he is doing a disservice to many of the Latinx students in his class.

Mr. Potts: And yeah, then you go, "maybe you're not hitting all the kids' reading levels. You should have them reading books that range from K-6." But then you also have little kids that I'm going, OK, if I do that, where does that put Mario? Where does that put Cassandra? Where does that put Yarely? Kids that got geared into my track, not by parental choice, but by teachers bringing in kids that couldn't succeed anywhere else. Suddenly David and Sarah and Brian read higher than them in Spanish and English. So, what have I done? When they were in another classroom, and they had to go to another group in the corner, it was "oh, it's because they're Spanish speakers". Their language is an excuse. Now I've stripped them of their excuse. They're low in both. The English kid can out do them in both environments. And then I go, "I've done them a disservice". Although the excuse was a lie, I let them hold face. They had the excuse that "the reason that I'm not doing well, is because I'm having to learn another language". And now they don't have that, because David or Sarah or Brian can say, "so are we, and we can read your language better than you can." And it makes it really tough.

In this interview, Mr. Potts contemplates whether he truly serves the Latinx, Spanish-dominant students better in his class or if they would fare better in a mainstream, English-instructed classroom where their status of being a language learner can mask some of the other issues that serve as barriers to their education, namely race and poverty. From these data, it becomes clear that Mr. Potts' attempts at implementing a dual language model in his classroom were not sufficient to protect the Latinx students from the effects of language ideologies that define them as deficient and begins to reveal why Mr. Potts believes, under these conditions, he is not an effective teacher.

Needless to say, Mr. Potts' stand-alone dual language class is not ideal by any means. This finding, however, does not mean that Mr. Potts' attempts at Latinx student advocacy were futile. As I move on to examine Mr. Potts' pedagogical practices, I find that there are both possibilities and impossibilities in his multicultural agenda to advocate for Latinx students. In the next section, I discuss Mr. Potts' contradictory pedagogical practices, beginning with what I consider his promising practices.

MR. POTTS' PROMISING PRACTICES

In Mr. Potts' makeshift dual language classroom, I found many examples of what I consider successful multicultural practices. In this section, I highlight these practices, which I title: Poetry Contests, Multiplying by Eleven, Stop the Stigma, and Parent-Teacher Conferences.

Poetry Contests

In a school system that is defined by language ideologies that undermine the Spanish language, Mr. Potts often sought out small windows of opportunity to advocate for his Latinx students. In this example, Mr. Potts took advantage of the ambiguous rules of various poetry contests and submitted his Latinx, Spanish-speaking students' Spanish poems to poetry contests that were intended for English language submissions only. Nowhere in the rules and regulations of the contests was it written that poems needed to be submitted in a particular language. However, given the normative status of the English language, no mention of language at all can be assumed to mean English only. Mr. Potts took advantage of the rules' normative vagueness when it comes to language by submitting the poems his Latinx, Spanish-dominant students wrote in Spanish, along with the poems his white, English-dominant students wrote in English. While Mr. Potts' intention in submitting his students' poems in their native languages was to have them evaluated and to bring attention to the outstanding poems that were being written in both languages, the outcomes of his poem submissions were less than desired. Mr. Potts explains the results of this practice in an interview:

> The students who wrote in English received response letters and the children who wrote in Spanish didn't receive any recognition whatsoever. Not even a response that theirs had been sent, which bothered me immensely, because I went back to the rules and there was nothing that said that it had to be written in English.

With this one bad experience, Mr. Potts decided to be proactive when he submitted his students' poems to another poetry contest. Mr. Potts explains:

> With another contest which is right in the school, I called Washington DC, and asked the National PTA for the rules, what had to be done, cause I already had this one bad experience and they said that entering it in Spanish is just fine, but that I needed to go through and mark all of the mistakes in red, which first of all makes the Hispanic child's paper look worse than the Anglo child's paper, which I didn't like, and then provide a close as possible word for word translation at the bottom that would still convey the meaning. And in poetry word for word really stinks, but I did my best.

Despite following these newly formed rules for Spanish submissions, which he found inappropriate, the end result left Mr. Potts feeling discouraged and unsuccessful in bringing change to this system. Mr. Potts explains further:

> [In] last year's contest, they were thrown away. Uh, the judge at the school had assumed that the words used by the Spanish-speaking students were too high of a level. Uh, an example is the word '*subterraneo*' which means underground. And the close cognate I could come up with was subterranean and she was just positive that no fourth or fifth grade child would use the word subterranean. And so they just threw away all of my students' entries. So the following year I did not mass encourage my class. The first year—every single child in my class entered. The second year—I just went through and those kids who had some beautiful poetry on their own throughout the year, I said don't you want to enter this? And so, uh, Leticia, hers was the only one in Spanish entered.

So [Spanish entries] went from half the class to one. And when I translated it, I took it to two other teachers that both were Spanish speakers and had them verify and write on a note that it was translated [accurately] and that this was their original work. I never made a comment to the judges or the people in the PTA that I had went and done that, but hers was not only one of the winners in the school level, but it was the only one.

Although Mr. Potts' attempts to bring recognition to his Latinx students' work in Spanish was constrained by the assimilationist context in which he works, and that informed the poetry committee's evaluation process, there was some possibility in Mr. Potts' efforts to advocate for his Latinx students. In essence, Mr. Potts interrupted the poetry committee's unstated, and thus normative practice of only accepting and recognizing English poems as legitimate work. By interrupting a system that unofficially only recognizes English as an academic language, Mr. Potts pushed the poetry committee to come up with a process in which they would evaluate poems in Spanish, which ultimately brought recognition to one Latinx student's work.

Multiplying by Eleven

One of the benefits of placing linguistic minority students in dual language programs along side native English-speaking students is that linguistic minority students are perceived as knowledgeable and linguistically resourceful because they serve as language models and language brokers for their English-dominant peers. The positioning of Latinx, Spanish-dominant students as knowledgeable, even if temporarily in Mr. Potts' class, is evident when White, English-dominant students view the Latinx, Spanish-dominant students as linguistically resourceful. In Mr. Potts' class, Spanish-dominant students were often consulted by English-dominant students for translations during Spanish instruction. These translations provided by Spanish-dominant students proved critical to the White, English-dominant students' development in the Spanish language as well as their participation in class activities that were conducted in the Spanish language. An example of Latinx students' resourcefulness occurred during a math lesson when Mr. Potts was sharing a trick students can use when multiplying double-digit numbers by 11. Mr. Potts writes the following math problems on the board:

$$27 \quad 34$$
$$\underline{\times 11} \quad \underline{\times 11}$$

He then explains the strategy in English as he works through the problems on the board. Mr. Potts explains the first problem:

All you have to do when you're multiplying by 11 is lower the first number, 2, and put it on the left side of your answer. Then lower the next number, 7, and put it on the right side of your answer. Make sure and leave space in the middle for another number. Now add the two numbers, 2+7, and put their sum in the center. And that's the answer.

Mr. Potts continues on, solving the next math problem on the board and explaining the strategy in English. When he is done, he points to the two solved problems on the board:

```
  27      34
 X11     X11
 297     374
```

He then provides the students the opportunity to solve a problem on their own:

Mr. Potts: Okay, who thinks they can do one?

The students, who are always excited to learn a new math trick, anxiously wait for the chance to demonstrate that they can solve a problem. Those students who were able to follow along Mr. Potts' instructions in English extend their hands, waving them back and forth to get Mr. Potts' attention. A few students stand on their chairs and extend out their arms and hands as high as they can to try and catch Mr. Potts' attention. Unexpectedly, Mr. Potts switches over to Spanish and does not write anything on the board to facilitate English-dominant students' comprehension of what the new problems are.

Mr. Potts: Muy bien. Más dificil! Cuarenta y nueve por once (Alright. More difficult. 49x11).

Mr. Potts walks to the different tables where he awards each table of students points for providing the right answer to this math problem. Mr. Potts writes these points on the board where he already has a running tally of points for each table of students. These points can be redeemed later for awards, such as being released early for recess and even a class party. Mr. Potts proceeds to visit each table where any student from the table can whisper the answer into Mr. Potts' ear. Realizing that Mr. Potts will shortly approach his table, Brian, a White, English-dominant student, anxiously tries to figure out what Mr. Potts has said in Spanish so that he can get points for his table. He quickly turns to Julio—a Mexican, Spanish-dominant student at his table.

Brian: What did he say? What did he say?
Julio: Forty-nine times eleven.

Brian quickly writes down the problem on a piece of paper and is able to solve the problem before Mr. Potts arrives to their table. Brian provides the answer when Mr. Potts asks for it and gains points for his table. This is an example of when the students work together to obtain points for their table. Since the instructions were delivered in English, Julio may have not been able to fully comprehend how to solve the problem using the strategy Mr. Potts had instructed them to use. What was clear though is that Julio was positioned as knowledgeable in this context, because he was able to give the translation of the math problem, which ultimately led the entire table to get points.

In this class, even despite their perceived low-level status, Spanish-dominant students may be positioned as more linguistically adept than their English-dominant peers. As this example illustrates, the Spanish-dominant student was able to understand the problem in Spanish and translate it into English, thereby demonstrating fluency in both languages.

Stop the Stigma

Along with positioning Latinx, Spanish-speaking students as knowledgeable because of their fluency in the Spanish language, the dual language model also serves to alleviate the stigmatized status that many ELLs often endure when enrolled in segregated language programs.

Data that reflect this outcome did emerge in Mr. Potts' class. On one afternoon Mr. Potts required two students to stay in class during recess because they were talking and interrupting Mr. Potts while he was delivering a lesson to the class. Before Mr. Potts released the rest of the students for recess, he explained what he wanted those students who would be staying in class to do during their recess time.

Mr. Potts: Necesito un favor. Para los estudiantes que tienen su nombre en la pizarra blanca, necesito que escriban una hoja que dice que yo no debería hablar en clase y no voy a hablar en la clase. Van a llevar la hoja a sus padres para que firmen y si no la regresan, van a recibir un cheque, un cheque, y un cheque (I need a favor. For those students whose names are on the white board, I need a sheet of paper that says that I should not talk in class and I'm not going to talk in class. You're going to take the sheet of paper to your parents so they can sign it and if you do not return it, you're going to receive a check, a check, and a check).

During recess I stayed in class with these two students while Mr. Potts went out to the playground with the rest of his class. The two students who stayed behind were upset, and soon after Mr. Potts left, an argument erupted between the two boys (one White and one Mexican). The Mexican boy was upset with the White boy, blaming him for the situation they were in.

Mexican boy: This is your fault. You don't know how to listen.
White boy: You don't know how to speak English.
Mexican boy: You don't know how to speak Spanish.

Both boys became quiet and began writing. As can be noted, the White student employs a common put-down that stems from the language deficit ideology, which positions the Mexican student as linguistically deficient due to his lack of English fluency. However, since the White student is also learning a second language, the Mexican student quickly responds by pointing out the same deficiency in the White boy's target language: Spanish. As can be seen here, stigmatizing a Spanish-speaker while he or she is learning English loses some impact in a context where English-speakers are learning a second language and where they can be equally perceived as "lacking" language.

Parent-Teacher Conferences

Traditionally, parent-teacher conferences are scheduled individually with each child's parent(s) and it is not necessary that the child attends the conference. In contrast to this traditional method of scheduling parent-teacher conferences, Mr. Potts doubles up his conference appointments by simultaneously scheduling one White, English-dominant student with one Latinx, Spanish-dominant student along with their parent(s). During each conference, Mr. Potts asks the students to demonstrate some of what they have learned in class so that parents can observe their child's progress in content as well as their language comprehension.

Part of the content Mr. Potts asks students to display during this meeting is their ability to recite the multiplication table (0 through 12) in 60 seconds or less, which grants the students status as "60-second-club members". Mr. Potts has the English-dominant students recite the times table in English and the Spanish-dominant students recite it in Spanish and then vice versa. The purpose of the recitations is so that the parents can understand the students in their home language, but also so parents can have a sense of how the students are performing in their target language.

The genius of the parent-teacher conferences are not the fact that parents observe the academic skills of their own children, but rather that the White, English-monolingual parent(s) have the opportunity to observe the Latinx, Spanish-dominant students perform academically. The overwhelming response by White, English-monolingual parents at these conferences is that they are surprised and impressed that a Spanish-dominant child knows the equivalent of what their child knows, but in the Spanish language; in terms of fluency in the target languages, the Spanish-dominant child actually outperforms the White, English dominant child. In an interview, Mr. Potts addresses his approach to parent-teacher conferences:

> Mr. Potts: They hear each other's conferences. And Lupe will get up there and be able to do the 60-second-club and be able to do everything that I'm asking Frank to do, whether she does it in English or Spanish, and the parents are impressed. And then they [students] do the translation sheet. Maybe their [white parents'] child will struggle on doing it in the opposite direction, but the Spanish student might fly right through. And they [the parents] are like, "Wow!"

If Mr. Potts was to simply follow the traditional parent-teacher conference protocol in terms of scheduling one child at a time, the status quo of the language deficit ideology would be maintained. Mr. Potts' transformative practice, however, challenges White parents' often deficit perceptions of Latinx students—perceptions that lead parents to think that the Latinx, Spanish-dominant students potentially hold their White, English-dominant children behind in what is supposed to be an advanced learning experience. Indeed, Mr. Potts' unique way of organizing parent-teacher conferences serves to interrupt the dominant perception among many of the White, English-monolingual parents that the Latinx, Spanish-dominant students within the class are not as academically adept as their children. After attending the parent-teacher conferences, there was little discussion amongst White, English-monolingual parents that suggested the Spanish-dominant students may be holding the class back, thereby preventing their children from reaching their full potential. On the contrary, several White, English monolingual parents discussed the Latinx students' high academic performance.

In this section, I have elaborated on several pedagogical practices that indicate the promise in Mr. Potts' advocacy for Latinx students. As I discussed in chapter one, however, ideal conceptions of multicultural teaching are impossible to actualize with any consistency. In the following section, I highlight the contradictory nature of Mr. Potts' pedagogical practices within his larger agenda of Latinx advocacy. In the discussion that follows, I identify some of the ways in which Mr. Potts' advocacy for Latinx educational achievement go astray.

LATINX ADVOCACY IN PERIL

Due to the prevailing language ideologies as well as the overall privileging of White, English-dominant students at Viewpoint Elementary (White superiority ideology), there are a number of ways in which the stand-alone dual language model became derailed in Mr. Potts' classroom. As the data in this section show, Mr. Potts' pedagogical practices sometimes worked against his multicultural goals by privileging White, English-dominant students—students who had already been singled out for being bright kids who can handle learning a second language. As will be seen in this section, these are the very students who receive the most specialized instruction aimed to foster their language development as well as access to core curriculum. The sections that follow are titled: Translation Sheets, English Reigns, Sheltered Spanish, and Using Spanish as a Tool for Instruction.

Translation Sheets

In addition to receiving teacher referrals, many of the White, English-dominant students' parents highly encouraged their children to enroll in Mr. Potts' class so that they can take advantage of the "advanced" language program that provides them the opportunity to learn a second language. However, as I explained in the discussion on parent-teacher conferences, these parents are aware that the class contains teacher-identified, "low-level" Latinx students, which makes them cautious as to whether the Latinx, Spanish-dominant students slow down the curriculum and language development of their White children. Because the White, English-monolingual parents do not speak Spanish themselves, there is no way for them to gauge through conversation with their children, whether they are indeed learning Spanish. As a result, several White parents have demanded that Mr. Potts produce some kind of indicator that shows that their children are learning Spanish. In this case, the parents are invoking the ideology of White superiority. That is, White students' education, and in this case proof they are learning Spanish, comes to take precedence over other activities and outcomes that may be important to Latinx students and their parents. Mr. Potts makes clear that White, English-monolingual parents' demands for a formal indicator of Spanish language development constrains his pedagogical practices. Mr. Potts talks about this process in an interview.

> Mr. Potts: Well, when they [White children learning Spanish] get home, the kids don't use it [Spanish]. I mean, yeah, the Spanish-speaking kids will go home and still use English because it's in the environment all around them. My English-speaking kids go home and there's not a call for them to use Spanish, and so the parents don't realize, and originally I tried the little books, like the kindergarten teachers have, but I had to borrow them from other teachers and they would get lost and then I would have to reimburse the teachers and it wasn't often enough. I could borrow it for maybe a week or two-week period of time, but parents needed something nightly, that we're showing growth, that we're showing progress. So I came up with the translation sheets.

Feeling the pressure to demonstrate White students' Spanish skills, Mr. Potts implemented a pedagogical practice that he calls "translation sheets". These sheets are worksheets he develops that contain a series of vocabulary words and then corresponding sentences (either in English or Spanish) that include the vocabulary words. Students are to translate the vocabulary words and sentences, often during class time, and then take the sheet home for parents to look over and sign.

Even though Mr. Potts uses the translation sheets to highlight students' ability to translate in both languages, and even incorporates a demonstration of students' ability to complete the translation sheets into the parent-teacher conference sessions, he is highly critical of this practice. Mr. Potts expresses his frustration over the translation sheets and how this practice contradicts the dual language model:

> Mr. Potts: I mean, to be an actual dual language class I couldn't translate at all and yet I give assignments to the kids to translate, which is totally against what you're supposed to do. But I'm going,

"I don't know how to make things work and I'm struggling and trying to do what I feel is best".

Within the sociopolitical context in which Mr. Potts is embedded, he is pressured into producing a pedagogical practice that privileges White students and parents. This pedagogical practice not only privileges White students by providing a formal indicator of their learning but takes valuable time away from curriculum development, class preparation, and class time. In the end, Mr. Potts believes that this pedagogical practice hinders both Latinx, Spanish-dominant students' and White, English-dominant students' learning experiences.

English Reigns

As much as he can, Mr. Potts tries to follow the 50/50 model of dual language instruction, which divides instruction time in half, delivering 50 percent of instruction in English and 50 percent in Spanish. In a traditional dual language program, two teachers would carry out the division of instruction. One teacher would deliver English instruction and another teacher would deliver Spanish instruction, and two classes of dual language students would switch between the two teachers who follow a rigid 50/50 allocation of language instruction without any translating. Given that Mr. Potts is not in a dual language program, he must deliver both English and Spanish instruction to his students. As such, Mr. Potts' language allocation is not only rough, it actually favors the English language more. Moreover, his uneven language instruction conflicts with the placement of the students in Mr. Potts' class. As discussed previously, whereas the White, English-dominant students are placed in Mr. Potts' class because they have already demonstrated English fluency and superior academic performance, Latinx, Spanish-dominant students are placed in Mr. Potts' class because of a perceived academic deficiency. As a result of the student placement strategies utilized in Mr. Potts' class, it would make more sense to give priority to Spanish instruction. This strategy would make sense for both sets of students. The White, English-dominant students not only can supposedly handle instruction in a second language, they need more exposure to the Spanish language, given their immersion in English language contexts outside of class. For Spanish-dominant students, native language development is linked to increased access to and achievement in the core curriculum, as well as fostering second language (English) development (Cummins, 1996). Thus, by increasing Spanish instruction time, Spanish-dominant students would find the curriculum more accessible and they would increase their fluency in both the Spanish and English languages. However, the seemingly logical pedagogical practice of delivering more Spanish instruction than English instruction does not surface in Mr. Potts' class.

Mr. Potts admits to favoring the White, English-dominant students by delivering his instruction mostly in English. Mr. Potts tells me that he only speaks Spanish for roughly 30 percent of his instruction time, because there is concern in the school about the "advanced" English-dominant kids falling behind in curriculum due to the potential language barrier in Mr. Potts' class. Clearly fitting the ideology of White superiority, Mr. Potts feels pressured to ensure English-dominant students not fall behind in curriculum.

Here we see that unlike established dual language models that strategically and strictly divide language instruction either by subject matter, time of day, or day of week, Mr. Potts uses no particular pattern for delivering instruction in English and Spanish (as was evidenced in the previously discussed math lesson). While he tries to deliver an entire lesson in one language, either English or Spanish, he often unconsciously breaks code. In my observations, I noticed Mr. Potts uses Spanish instruction intermittently, usually maintaining the 30/70 ratio of language distribution. For example, in the following passage, Mr. Potts tries to calm students down as he gets them ready to end the school day.

> Mr. Potts: This day is going really bad. I have a really good class, but we're having a really bad day. Your ticket to go home. Tu boleto para ir a su casa, your ticket to go home is you need to write all the correct answers before you go.

By using English as the primary language in his instruction, one can see that Mr. Potts often caters to the educational achievement of White, English-dominant students, thereby enabling the white superiority ideology.

Sheltered Spanish

Mr. Potts delivers instruction primarily in English so that White, English-dominant students have access to the curriculum in the language they are stronger in. In further support of ensuring English-dominant students' accessibility to instruction, Mr. Potts also makes provisions in his Spanish language instruction. In this case, Mr. Potts often uses what can be called sheltered Spanish when he addresses the class in Spanish. The equivalent to sheltered Spanish in English instruction is called sheltered English, which occurs when an instructor who is teaching English to ELLs accompanies speech with very animated, nonverbal gestures as well as props to facilitate students' language comprehension. The benefit of using sheltered English is that students do not rely on decontextualized speech alone to understand English instruction. Rather, students couple speech with nonverbal communication to gain comprehension of the lesson at hand. In my participant-observations of Mr. Potts' pedagogical practices, I made note several times that Mr. Potts uses very little sheltered English when addressing the class in English, but regularly uses sheltered Spanish when he addresses the class in Spanish. One such example of sheltered Spanish occurred on a morning after he had been absent from class. On this morning, Mr. Potts explains to the students in Spanish how his day away from school went. Along with Mr. Potts' statements in Spanish, I describe his use of sheltered Spanish in the following passage.

Mr. Potts: Yo tenía que ir al corte ayer para transducir. Yo estaba tan nervioso [tensing his body and widening his eyes to illustrate his nervousness to the students] que no pensé a mirar mi gasolina [sitting on a chair in front of the class, acting like he's driving a car, Mr. Potts positions his hands in the air in front of him like they're on a steering wheel and moving them back and forth like he is steering a car. Mr. Potts points to where the gasoline gauge would be inside the car and extends his index finger out and moves it from side to side to indicate to the students that he's talking about a gauge that moves from side to side], y se paró mi carro en la carretera [Mr. Potts jerks back and forth in his seat and then suddenly stops moving altogether to indicate that the car jumped around a bit and then finally came to a complete stop]. Yo comencé corriendo en la carretera con mi dedo arriba [Mr. Potts acts like he's opened the car door, stands up from the chair, and begins running back and forth in front of the class with his thumb extended up in the air]. Paró un auto y adentro era una señora con tres niños [runs back over to the chair and acts like he's opening the car door and getting into the lady's car. Once seated on the chair, Mr. Potts points to where the driver would be and holds up one finger to indicate one lady and then turns his head around to where the back seat would be and holds up three fingers to indicate three children]. Me bajó en la escuela [gets off the chair again to indicate that he is getting out of the car]. La directora de la escuela me dio un rite al corte [sitting in the chair again to indicate that he's in a car again], gracias a ella, y [alguien de la escuela] se fue para mi carro.

Without the use of sheltered Spanish, here is Mr. Pott's message translated into English:

I had to go to court yesterday to translate. I was so nervous that I didn't think to look at my gasoline, and my car died on the freeway. I started running on the freeway with my thumb up. A car stopped and inside was a lady with three children. She dropped me off at school. The school principal gave me a ride to court, thanks to her, and (someone from the school) went for my car.

As indicated in this example of sheltered Spanish, students can gain meaning from Mr. Potts' discussion by paying attention to his body gestures and props, such as the chair he uses to represent a seat in a car. His use of sheltered Spanish for the English-dominant students, as well as his minimal use of sheltered English with Spanish-dominant students, once again privileges the White, English-dominant students' educational experiences, thereby illustrating the impact the White superiority ideology has on his pedagogical practices.

Spanish as a Tool for Instruction

The purpose of a "true" dual language program is for students to become fully bilingual and biliterate as two target languages are taught through the content. In this design, both languages are treated as academic and worthy of learning as they are incorporated into academic content students must learn. In contrast to this goal, however, Mr. Potts' pedagogical practices sometimes involve a practice in which he uses Spanish as a tool for instructing content rather than as academic content in and of itself. Perhaps unintentional, the outcomes of this pedagogical practice are: 1) the establishment of the English language as the only academic language, 2) the relegation of the Spanish language as an expendable language, and 3) the rendering of White, English-dominant students as more academically astute than Spanish dominant students. An example of how this pedagogical practice plays out is when Mr. Potts instructs an assignment in which students must write a haiku using information they previously learned about the U.S. government. Mr. Potts begins his lesson by defining a haiku as a Japanese poem with three lines.

> Mr. Potts: The first line has five syllables. The second line has seven syllables, and the third line has five syllables. You're going to be writing a haiku on the U.S. government.

Mr. Potts illustrates a few examples by writing them on the board, sounding out each syllable, so that students can make note of the 5, 7, 5 syllable pattern. Mr. Potts writes on the board:

Executive Branch 5

Headed by the President 7

He can veto bills 5

Mr. Potts then begins the lesson in Spanish, at which point the English-dominant students tune out Mr. Potts' instruction to begin writing their haikus.

> Mr. Potts: Ahora en español. Haiku es un tipo de poema Japonese. Por ejemplo puede ser …(Now in Spanish. Haiku is a type of Japanese poem. For example, it can be…) [Mr. Potts writes on the board]:

Veo la rosa 5 (I see the rose)

Que bella en el jardín 7 (How beautiful in the garden)

Color del amor 5 (Color of love)

> Mr. Potts: Ahora, la única que quiero es que escribes un haiku del gobierno, no de rosas. (Now, the only thing I want is that you write a haiku about the government, not about roses.)

Mr. Potts then illustrates some examples by writing two haikus on the government in Spanish on the board:

Poder judicia 5 (Judicial power)
Interpretan las leyes 7 (They interpret the laws)
Corte suprema 5 (Supreme court)

En el congreso 5 (In congress)
Juntos hacen los leyes 7 (Together they make the laws)
Las dos cámaras 5 (The two chambers)

By the time Mr. Potts finishes explaining the lesson in Spanish and before the Spanish-dominant students begin to write their own haikus, many of the White, English dominant students have completed the task of writing a haiku. In fact, at the precise moment Mr. Potts finishes explaining the lesson in Spanish, Scott, one of the White, English-dominant students, gets up from his table to show Mr. Potts his completed haiku. Mr. Potts reads Scott's haiku to himself and then reads it out loud to the class, announcing that it is a good example of a haiku on government and then praises Scott for his work. The class applauses Scott's work and then Scott sits down at his table. Two other White, English-dominant students follow Scott's lead by coming up to Mr. Potts so that he can read their haikus as well. Content with their work, Mr. Potts reads these haikus out loud in front of the class as well, and the class once again applauds the work the students have done. The last bell of the day rings and Mr. Potts announces to the class that if they have not finished writing their haikus, they can take them home and finish them for homework. The class is then released for the day.

In a traditional dual language program, teachers would not translate lessons or assignments as Mr. Potts has done in this lesson. Rather, the entire lesson would be delivered in one language—either English or Spanish (most commonly from different teachers), and students work to achieve comprehension in the language of instruction as well as the content of the lesson. In Mr. Potts' stand-alone dual language class, he is responsible for delivering instruction in both languages, and as this example as well as others illustrate, he sometimes changes the language of instruction in the middle of a lesson. Important in this example with the haiku lesson is that Mr. Potts has delivered the lesson in the two languages in an effort to reach and address the two linguistic audiences in his class separately. Further, even though Mr. Potts does not commonly translate lessons from one language to another, when he does, he almost always delivers the lesson in English first.

In this example, English is treated as the only academic language. Because the lesson is delivered in English first, the White, English-dominant students do not pay attention to the Spanish version of the lesson, but instead begin to do the academic work. The "academic work" in this case, is narrowed to writing a haiku, not learning Spanish. Likewise, the Latinx, Spanish-dominant students in this case learn that

Spanish is not part of the academic agenda, but rather just a tool for instructing the "real" academic content. By translating the lesson into Spanish, and only for the purpose of teaching the Spanish dominant students, Spanish is treated only as a means to comprehend the lesson (writing a haiku) that had already been instructed in English. Using Spanish as a tool for instruction, rather than academic content, sends the message that the Spanish language is expendable in the schooling context. Once the Spanish-dominant students become fluent in English, Spanish foreseeably would no longer serve a purpose in classroom instruction. Another important outcome of Mr. Potts delivering the lesson in English first, which obviously supports the English first ideology, is that English-dominant students are afforded the opportunity to finish their work before Spanish-dominant students even have a chance to begin their work, which in this case results in Mr. Potts praising English-dominant students' academic work. Using Spanish as a tool for instruction instead of as the content of instruction demonstrates how Mr. Potts' pedagogical practices often reinforce the racial status quo by privileging White students.

CONCLUDING REMARKS

Important to this analysis is to understand that Mr. Potts' multicultural practices are anything but monolithic. He is neither a multicultural hero nor defender of the status quo. Rather, he is both. This case study shows that even though Mr. Potts delivers transformative multicultural practices, he also reinforces the power dynamics that privileges the White, English-dominant students in his class. Thus, it is not helpful to conceptualize Mr. Potts' pedagogical practices as wholly ideal and/or antiracist, as this perception strips away the complexity and contradictory nature of Mr. Potts' pedagogical practices in a racially charged school and social context.

MS. DEGRAW'S ESL CLASSROOM

It is first period in Ms. DeGraw's English as a Second Language (ESL) class and today there is a guest speaker who will be speaking about careers and life planning. Ms. Short, the ESL counselor at Drew Middle School (DMS) will be delivering the presentation. As Ms. DeGraw marks the daily attendance, Mrs. Short explains to the class that they will be learning about life's major events and what it takes to make ends meet by playing a fun board game.

Mrs. Short: Hello Everyone. Today we are going to talk about your futures. I want you to be prepared for your futures and think about how you can make a living by doing something you really like doing. Take my husband, for example. He makes furniture for a living. He makes something with his hands that is beautiful and then he sells it for a lot of money. Today we are going to talk about your lives. In order to do this, I need you to take everything off your tables and I need five to six people per table. Ok, you need to listen. There are going to be instructions. You're going to be able to earn money to buy candy. Whoever gets to the final spot on the board first at your table wins the big prize. You're going to play a game, kind of like Monopoly. You may land on "have a baby" and you will owe $20,000. If you don't have it, then you get an IOU from the bank and if you land on that again then you owe $40,000. You might land on a space that tells you that your rent has gone up $700.00 and you have to pay it every time you land on it.

Before the students even begin to play the game, Ms. DeGraw comes to me to voice her frustration about the game:

Ms. DeGraw: I am appalled. These people don't have a clue about real life for these students. There are things on there [the game board] that says "Your car broke down, no insurance, now you have to take the bus". It's like they haven't got a clue on the needs of these students.

After Mrs. Short finishes explaining the instructions, she assigns an adult to each table of students, including herself, Ms. DeGraw, Mrs. Richardson (the school principal), and two other adult visitors to help facilitate the game. Soon after, the students begin to play the game by spinning a wheel, which either tells them "free candy" or a number to indicate how many spaces to move on the board. The board has many spaces, organized to create a road to the final winning spot. The first person to reach the end of the road wins a big candy bar. Each space on the board has a statement as well as corresponding directions, such as pay, receive money, move forward so many spaces, or move backward so many spaces. As I walk around the room and observe the game in process, I notice that Ms. DeGraw is having a difficult time facilitating the game. She makes faces, sighs, and shrugs her shoulders as she tries to understand the significance of the messages her ESL students struggle to read in English. Ms. DeGraw's frustration escalates when she tries to communicate the meaning of the messages to her students. For example, when Leticia lands on the space, "You are in jail and have an arrest record," she sounds out the English words but does not understand their meaning. Ms. DeGraw then intervenes by acting out the message for Leticia. Ms. DeGraw grips the air in front of her face with her two hands and then sticks her head in the space in between her two clenched fists, as if gripping jail bars and looking through the bars. Ms. DeGraw leans over to me and expresses her anger.

Ms. DeGraw: I don't know how to tell her that she is in jail and has an arrest record. This is so ridiculous!

As Ms. DeGraw continues to facilitate the game at her table, she soon begins to modify the meaning of the messages and eventually deletes the messages altogether, simply telling students how many spaces to move or how much money to collect or pay. As students continue to play the game, they land on a number of spaces, some of which read as follows:

Old cellmate from jail comes to see you, borrows $100,000.
Factory closed down, go back five spaces.
Joined gang, wanted in a police line-up, lose two turns.
Get out of jail, lose your job because of arrest record.
Get married, no education. Have to live with parents.
Baby born, no insurance, pay $20,000.

During this process, it is evident to me, and Ms. DeGraw confirms later, that Ms. DeGraw is angry over the stereotypical life roles that are depicted on the board game and assumed to represent her seventh-grade ESL students' futures. In a frustrated tone, Ms. DeGraw tells me:

Ms. DeGraw: I guarantee you they do not have the neighborhood kids (White students) at this school playing this game. They [people administering this game] are so damn racist!

After the game ended and Mrs. Short and the other adults leave the room, Ms. DeGraw shows signs of relief that they are finally gone. However, she continues to nonverbally express her dislike for the presentation. Organizing papers at her desk, she mumbles to herself a number of unintelligible remarks. I ask Ms. DeGraw what continues to anger her. Among her many complaints about the presentation, she immediately brings up Ms. Short and the comments she made about her husband:

Ms. DeGraw: On top of everything else, I hate it when other people talk about their husbands and wives in public…like nothing. They are so privileged and they don't even realize it! I never get to talk about my partner at this school. My students know nothing about her.

Ms. DeGraw then walks to the front of the class to address with her students some of the other issues she had with the presentation:

Ms. DeGraw: How many people won the game? Levantense sus manos (Raise your hands).

Ms. DeGraw counts as she stands in front of the class and points to raised hands.

Ms. DeGraw: 1,2,3,4,5. About 20 people did not win the game. Do you think that's true of life? Do you think only five people will be successful in here? Also, do you think money is the only way to be successful? Look at me. I have a house. I have children. I have a good job. I get to be with you. You don't need to have a lot of money to have a good life. You just have to do what you like. So if you want to be a teacher and you think, no, not enough money, no! It's a good life. If you had a good time playing this game that's good, but I don't want you to think that money means everything in life. It's only one thing. I believe all of you will be successful, regardless of the amount of money you will make.

I open Ms. DeGraw's case study with this field observation, because I think it is a good representation of the advocacy work that defines her multicultural practices. As this class activity on "careers" and "life-planning" shows, Ms. DeGraw is very critical of how her ESL students are treated at DMS. She is aware of the many negative ideologies that define her students and their schooling experiences. As the above data demonstrate, Ms. DeGraw attempts to restrict the flow of these ideologies by silencing them or pointing them out and deconstructing their implicit meanings with her students. When her students were playing the board game, Ms. DeGraw was critical of the messages on the game board, which interestingly enough never highlighted any career options for the students, but rather presumptions about how the students' lives would be filled with careless behaviors that will inevitably result in undesired consequences, including unplanned pregnancies, bankruptcy, and jail time. She also disliked the message that suggested that all of her students could not be successful, regardless of their future incomes. While the students were playing the game, Ms. DeGraw interrupted these messages by serving as a buffer between the negative messages and her students. After noting the negative tone that the messages inflicted on her students, and knowing her students did not fully understand the messages they were attempting to read in English, Ms. DeGraw began to eliminate the messages altogether, and instead, simply told the students what they needed to do in order to proceed in playing the game (e.g., how many spaces to move). Further, Ms. DeGraw tried to challenge the racist assumptions incorporated in the game by addressing them with her students. While some of her students may have enjoyed playing the game, as they were rewarded for doing so in the form of candy bars, she pushed her students to be critical of the messages that the game communicated.

As the opening to this case study demonstrates, Ms. DeGraw's multicultural practices are complex. While she does challenge the racist ideologies that define ESL students at DMS, it is unclear what effect her advocacy has on the major stakeholders in this schooling context, including the ESL counselor, principal, teachers, students, school district, and community. Also bringing complexity to Ms. DeGraw's advocacy work is that at the same time she advocates for her ESL students, which often means bringing visibility to the ESL students' presence at DMS, Ms. DeGraw's own lesbian identity is treated as taboo, pushing her to keep her "othered" identity invisible and silent. Consistent with the central theme of this book, Ms. DeGraw's multicultural practices are not always triumphant. Much like Mr. Potts' case study, Ms. DeGraw's multicultural practices resemble the (im) possibilities of the multicultural teacher.

MS. DEGRAW'S CRITICAL PERSPECTIVE

Ms. DeGraw's critical, multicultural perspective and overall intensity in addressing social justice issues stem from her own life experiences. During one-on-one interviews, Ms. DeGraw often elaborated on how she feels oppressed as a woman, especially in her relationships with her father, ex-husband, and colleagues.

> Ms. DeGraw: Being marginalized definitely has made me understand what marginalization feels like. Um, and just how important it is for people to know that they have a voice, because for so long I didn't know that I had a voice. My voice did not express itself at all, because my father said it doesn't count and my ex-husband said the same thing. [My ex-husband] totally minimized me because I was female, totally. [He] told me at one point that he didn't think I was bright. It's just like totally, I mean that's like, I can't tell you how surprised I was, let alone hurt and angry and shocked and surprised that he didn't understand that about me, that he didn't know I was bright. How could you not, you know, how did he not know that about me?

Along with feeling voiceless most of her life as a woman, Ms. DeGraw adds that she continues to feel voiceless in many situations currently because of her lesbian identity. Afraid of jeopardizing her job, Ms. DeGraw does not reveal her sexual identity at work. In the city where DMS is located, politicians are primarily White conservative men, of the dominant religion, and openly anti-gay. Ms. DeGraw tells me she finds it very difficult to live in this environment.

> Ms. DeGraw: I just never cease to be amazed by how anti-gay this place [city] is. It's just blatant anti-gay and legislative sessions are always just full of real hard stuff. It's hard. It's hard to be part of this, part of this culture [lesbian] and not be recognized for who I am. I just get outraged by how much power they [White heterosexual men] have.

Ms. DeGraw further explains that her experiences with oppression motivate her to work as an activist for her students, who are marginalized for their race, ethnicity, language, and immigration status (many of whom are refugees).

> Ms. DeGraw: I think growing up here, and being, you know, kind of exotic here in this culture, being outside the dominant [straight] culture, has always given me, um, has always made me want to have a voice and make sure that other people that don't have a voice get heard. I think that's probably a huge part of what happened, of why I feel the way I do. Growing up in a dominant straight culture that I'm not part of, um, you know, where opening the paper can send me in a tizzy, because it's such an outrage about how much religious life dominates life in this community, that I want people that aren't part of that to know that they, that they count, and that they need to stand up and speak for themselves and that they need to, um oppose, you know, oppose stuff that that, that, what's the word I want? That puts them down and keeps them down.

As indicated in this interview, Ms. DeGraw's experiences with oppression feed her desire to work as an activist for her students at DMS.

DREW MIDDLE SCHOOL

DMS is located in the city's upper east side. Whereas Viewpoint Elementary (where Mr. Potts teaches) is located on the West side of town where poor and ethnic minorities live, Ms. DeGraw lives and teaches on the East side of town where the residents are almost entirely White and middle-upper class. Roughly 750 seventh- and eighth-grade students attend DMS. Some 20 years ago, the school developed a magnet ESL program for the middle school ELLs in the district. The program started off small, bussing in only 50 ELLs from the west side of town to this prestigious White suburb school. Now, two decades later, the school busses in 272 of their 309 ELLs who in all, make up 41 percent of the school's population and who come from 37 countries and speak 21 different languages. Ms. DeGraw teaches seventh- and eighth-grade students in the school's magnet ESL program. In this specific schooling context where ELLs participate in the school's ESL program, they are referred to as ESL students. For the sake of staying consistent with the terminology of the school, I refer to this student population as ESL students in this chapter.

SOCIOPOLITICAL CONTEXT

The sociopolitical context at DMS can best be described as assimilationist, and this is most obvious in the language program this school has implemented. ESL programs, by design, are assimilationist. The goal of ESL programs is to promote English language development through English language instruction. Native language maintenance and development are nonexistent in the goals of ESL programs. By adopting and implementing the ESL model to language development, DMS in effect pushes students to assimilate to the dominant White cultural and linguistic norm of the school, state, and larger U.S. society.

The very presence of ESL students on this campus is a contradictory affair. On the one hand, the school district has made a move toward integrating students by bussing ESL students into what is otherwise considered an elite White school within the district. On the other hand, ESL students are separated from the larger school by being placed in ESL classes and many other classes that are designated for ESL students. In this section I identify and explain how specific racial and linguistic ideologies define the sociopolitical context at DMS. These ideologies include: (1) ESL students are criminal, (2) ESL students are nuisances, and (3) ESL students are to be made invisible. In the following sections, I highlight the various players that are embedded within the sociopolitical context at DMS. These players include the teachers, students, community, principal, and school district.

Teachers

While racial ideologies often manifest in subtle ways, at other times they can be iterated in blunt terms. Ms. DeGraw's ESL students often come to her to report various instances of racism they experience with teachers in their other classes. On these occasions, Ms. DeGraw not only provides opportunities for her ESL students to talk about these incidents in one-on-one and whole-class discussions, but she often follows through and addresses the issue with the accused teacher, without identifying who reported the incident to her. In my casual conversations with Ms. DeGraw, she often shared these incidents with me. On one such occasion, Ms. DeGraw tells me about Mr. Chase, who is the choir teacher at DMS. Mr. Chase teaches two ESL choir classes as well as several other choir classes for the White, English monolingual students attending this school. Mr. Chase separates the ESL students from the White, English monolingual students in his choir classes, because as he explains, "ESL students cannot sing". Further, he does not allow ESL students to participate in after-school choir productions that are presented to family, friends, and the larger community. Ms. DeGraw explains that Mr. Chase openly states that

ESL students are not allowed to participate in choir productions, because they bring down the quality of the productions. Ms. DeGraw responds to the exclusion of ESL students from choir productions in an interview:

I was very bothered by the fact that at our assembly in December—the Christmas, quote unquote holiday assembly—um was all about White faces on the stage. All the kids who were performing were White. Forty percent of the school population is kids of color and there was not one of these kids on stage. And the fact that it was all Christian. And all the songs were about Jesus. And it's about, you know, singing and dancing and, you know, who could not participate in that kind of thing? How could you not find a way for kids, for everybody to be part of that?

The exclusion of ESL students from choir productions as well as all other student performances and assemblies is an excellent example of how the ideology of invisibility functions at DMS. Even though ESL students make up nearly half of the student body at DMS and are active participants in their own choir classes, they are essentially invisible to the larger school and community, as these productions exclusively present the face of White, English monolingual students.

In addition to Mr. Chase, there are other teachers, such as Mr. Becker and Ms. Kline, who make racist comments in their classrooms. Mr. Becker is another ESL teacher, who teaches in the room right next to Ms. DeGraw. When the ESL students get in trouble in Mr. Becker's class, he has them write the phrase: "Mr. Becker will send me back to my country if I misbehave again". The students are required to write this statement several times on the white board as a form of punishment. Ms. Kline teaches health classes at DMS. In one particular class session at the beginning of the school year, Ms. Kline addresses her mixed White, English monolingual and ESL class about what they need to bring with them every day to her classroom. Among the several items that Ms. Kline emphasizes as being important to bring to class is a notebook. She then singles out the ESL students in her class by announcing in front of the class, "Now I know a lot of you from other countries have a hard time remembering things, so try and remember your notebooks". Part of Ms. DeGraw's advocacy work is that she encourages her students to voice these racist experiences in her class so that she can address them with the faculty, which she regularly does. Commonly after school, Ms. DeGraw is found in another teacher's classroom addressing specific comments and/or actions her students made her aware of, explaining to the teachers why such comments/actions are unacceptable.

Teachers' overall sentiments about the ESL students are also voiced in very clear terms at faculty meetings. In one particular meeting, teachers and administrators were talking about the projected dates of disassembling the ESL magnet program so that ESL students could go back to attending their neighborhood schools. During this meeting, many teachers expressed eagerness for the program to be disassembled, and a few teachers stated in very clear terms that if it did not happen soon, they would begin to look for work at another school.

49

Students

In addition to addressing the racist comments that teachers make, Ms. DeGraw regularly addresses the racist comments White, English monolingual students make. As I will explain shortly, Ms. DeGraw feels she is much less successful in her attempts to address racism with students. As Ms. DeGraw explains, the "neighborhood kids" often do not know how to interact with the ESL kids, and they often make inappropriate comments. While walking down the hallways between classes, for example, White students can be heard telling the ESL students to "go back to their country" and to "speak English". Ms. DeGraw discusses some of these incidents and her attempts at addressing them in an interview:

Ms. DeGraw: I was walking down the hall the other day and I heard a kid say real loud and he's a kid in the school who is very notorious and he was in my eighth period last semester, so I got to know him a little bit, and he's a pain. His name is Blaine. And I heard him say very loud at the front entrance of the school, something like, "Oh yeah, is this your first day in America?" And so I thought, what is that about in this school? That is not OK. I walked down further and I saw that he was talking to this group of popular girls who were headed down the hall, at which side they passed me and I heard one of them say, "Well, yeah, now I'm gonna, I'm just gonna start calling you African, OK. I'll just call you African". And I had no idea what they were talking about, and I let it go. I didn't say anything, but it got under my collar, so first I went to Blaine when I saw him later in the day, and I said, "I heard you say that, in the hall this morning" and I said "in this school, what are you thinking? There are people who are here for the first day in America and you know that. What are you thinking? Don't. Please don't say things like that". I just told him point blank, I do not want to hear that from you". And then the girls, one of the girls I approached her later in the day and said "I heard you say something about being African" and [she said] "I can't remember saying that". I mean she totally, she said she really didn't remember. She was part of the whole group, and she would have said, but she didn't remember. And I asked Peter Bradford, who is across the hall from me, who has all those students, 'cause I talk to him about them all the time. He'll tell me who's popular and who's not. Cause I have no clue. And he'll tell me all the stuff about the dominant White culture, cause I really want to know. I feel as an ESL teacher I don't see those girls, so I have no power with them. They do not have any respect for me. They will not even look at me. They totally ignore me… So, there are definitely issues between the neighborhood kids [White students] and the ESL teachers.

In Ms. DeGraw's attempts to advocate for her ESL students, it does not seem to matter that Ms. DeGraw is White, middle class, and lives in the White suburb just a few blocks away from the school, much like the White, English monolingual students who attend DMS. Ms. DeGraw believes that the White, English monolingual students marginalize her, because she does not teach most of them and she is physically isolated from White, English monolingual students because she teaches in the "ESL hallway" where all the ESL classes are located. To some extent, the ideology of invisibility also applies to Ms. DeGraw's experiences at DMS. For the most part, Ms. DeGraw is not visible to the White, English monolingual population at DMS. As Ms. DeGraw iterates in her interview, "…they do not have any respect for me. They will not even look at me. They totally ignore me".

Community

The surrounding community has also expressed a dislike for the ESL population at DMS. Some of the residents in the neighborhood have complained about the students hanging around after school and sitting on their lawns. A few of the residents of this community have enrolled in my multicultural education classes at the university. In these classes, they sometimes elaborate on how DMS is now infested with gang and criminal activity, and as a result, they have chosen to enroll their White children in another middle school within the district. While gang and criminal activity never surfaced in my data collection, the ideology of criminality nonetheless defines ESL students in this schooling context. As I explained in the opening of this case study, the ideology of criminality was also iterated in the board game the students played. Much of the surrounding community has come to believe that students of color who do not speak fluent English are synonymous with gang members and criminals, even when there is no evidence for making this parallel.

Mrs. Richardson (The Principal)

The principal is also a significant component to the sociopolitical context at DMS. At one faculty meeting, the principal explains to the teachers that DMS needs to become more competitive, because parents are shopping for schools and they largely base their decisions on schools' publicized test scores. Her discussion specifically centers on ESL students and standardized testing. Interestingly, while she discusses ESL students' poor performance on the standardized tests, it is actually the White community who are the focus of her discussion. In essence, her discussion revolves around what "they" [DMS teachers and administrators] need to do with the ESL students in order to safeguard the privileged positions the White people occupy in this neighborhood. The principal addresses the teachers:

> Mrs. Richardson: We are faced with the press advertising our test scores and parents shopping for schools. We have open enrollment here, so parents can choose to put their kids in any school they want. And so then we're faced with the fact that this school is not going to be competitive. The public school system is at risk. And how do we test the ESL students? They're going to test our ESL students and we're going to look awful. And I want to say to the people who live around here that they ought to care about all this, because we're going to lose our property value if this is not a good school.

In Ms. Richardson's plea to "care" about how ESL students perform on standardized tests, it is actually the White neighborhood community, where the principal and many of DMS teachers live, that she is most concerned about.

The principal refers to the school as being "at risk" and then proceeds to characterize the White privileged community as being "at risk," because their property value is in jeopardy of going down if White, middle-upper class parents begin to pull their students out of DMS and enroll them in another school due to the school's publicized test scores. Interestingly, the ideology of invisibility comes to play here once again. More specifically, the interests of ESL students in this discussion are invisible. Questions such as, how are ESL students and their families affected by low test scores?; Do ESL students stand to gain anything by increasing their test scores?; and What is at stake for ESL students if teachers simply teach to the test for the sake of obtaining better test scores? Instead of considering these and other questions that affect ESL students, the only way that ESL students are considered in Mrs. Richardson's discussion is by positioning them as the culprit for putting the White, privileged community "at risk". For it is the ESL students, especially when considering they make up 41 percent of the student population, and are not yet fluent in English, who significantly bring down the test scores at DMS.

The framing of ESL students as responsible for bringing down the status of the school and putting White people "at-risk" also brings to bare the ideology of ESL students being a nuisance. The presence of ESL students at DMS is considered to be a nuisance to the White residents, the principal and teachers included, in this White suburb, because ESL students' performance on standardized tests brings down the ranking of the school, thus putting the real estate market in this middle-upper class, White neighborhood in jeopardy. Simply put, if the ESL students were not bussed onto this campus, these problems would not exist. Derrick Bell's (1980) theory of interest convergence is relevant here. Interest convergence, according to Bell, occurs when White people support social justice issues only when they stand to gain from such an effort. Bell asserts that in these instances, there is a convergence between the interests of white people and the pursuit of racial justice. In the end, the racial transformative actions of White people serve to promote Whites' interests, and in extension, White privilege. At DMS, Mrs. Richardson is making the case that ESL students' higher academic performance in terms of standardized test scores means more property value, or more specifically, monetary value for White residents.

Much like the White teachers at Viewpoint Elementary (discussed in chapter two) chose not to implement a school-wide dual language program in an effort to secure their own White privilege, including job security and advocating for a system that keeps ELLs out of their classes and in non-integrated bilingual classes, teachers at DMS advocate for ELLs to return to their home schools, or at the very least, improve upon their test scores, not because it is in the best interest of the students, but because it is what is best for White teachers' property value.

School District

In keeping with the ideology of invisibility that renders ESL students invisible until they overcome their perceived cultural and linguistic "deficiencies", the school district has not developed an ESL curriculum for ESL students. That is, while the district puts time and effort into developing a curriculum for mainstream classes that are attended by non-ESL students, they put no time or effort into developing an ESL curriculum, which reinforces the idea that ESL students are to remain invisible to the schooling process, including curriculum development, until they learn English. The absence of an ESL curriculum in the ESL program at DMS makes it clear that it does not matter what ESL students do in Ms. DeGraw's class, so long as they learn English. Similar to the English first ideology I discussed in Mr. Potts' case study in chapter two, ESL students at DMS must gain English fluency and literacy before they can gain visibility in school activities that seemingly matter.

In my use of the concept of invisibility in this case study, I want to clarify that invisibility is different from colorblindness, which also aims to omit race as a relevant factor in a schooling context. As Thompson (1999) explains, colorblindness is "the refusal to 'see' race" (p. 141) in an effort to treat all students the same (i.e., we are all American or human). Underlying ideologies of colorblindness is the idea that non-White cultural ways of being are considered undesirable and thus are better off to be disregarded in a schooling context. By disregarding students' diverse ways of being, students of color become "just students" and are included in what is considered "race-neutral" schooling. Thus, colorblind perspectives aim to "include" students in school activities. My conception of the ideology of invisibility, on the other hand, omits students of color and linguistic minorities from participating in what are considered legitimate school activities. In this section, for example, I have discussed how ESL students are excluded, and thus made invisible in choir productions, holiday assemblies, mainstream classes that the White, English monolingual students attend, as well as curriculum development at the district level.

Overall, the sociopolitical context at DMS positions ESL students as nuisances to the school and community. According to the logic of the specific language and racial ideologies I have identified, it would be best if ESL students were to be removed from DMS, and until that happens, they are to be made invisible. I have taken the time to describe various aspects of the sociopolitical context at DMS in an effort to contextualize the (im)possibilities of Ms. DeGraw's multicultural practices. While working within this sociopolitical context, Ms. DeGraw attempts to advocate for her ESL students by (1) bringing visibility to their cultural, linguistic, and other lived experiences, and (2) confronting the oppressive nature of DMS. Similar to what transpired in Mr. Potts' classroom, Ms. DeGraw's multicultural practices are characterized by the (im)possibilities of multicultural education. Thus, despite Ms. DeGraw's best intentions and many successes at challenging the racial status quo, her pedagogical practices often result in micro-level changes.

MS. DEGRAW'S CLASS

Ms. DeGraw teaches two level-1 ESL classes and an elective video-recording class that is attended by all White, English monolingual students. The students are on a block schedule, so Ms. DeGraw has each of her Level-1 ESL classes for roughly 2 hours each day. The only classes that are not part of the block schedule at DMS are the elective classes, so Ms. DeGraw's video recording class lasts for roughly an hour. One of Ms. DeGraw's ESL classes contains 24 students and the other has 25 students. All of her students are recent immigrants to the U.S. and most have lived in the United States for less than 2 years. About two thirds of her students are from Latin American countries, primarily from Mexico, but also from Honduras, Guatemala, Peru, and Panama. The other third of her students are from various countries including Congo, Sudan, Bosnia, Kosovo, Albania, Russia, Iraq, China and Viet Nam. The range of English proficiency among the ESL students in Ms. DeGraw's classes is wide. Some students have just arrived to the United States and are beginning to learn some basic vocabulary, while others are enrolled in Ms. DeGraw's Level-1 ESL class for a second year and have begun to speak and write more confidently in the English language.

Unlike the invisibility that defines ESL students in the larger school context, they are anything but invisible in Ms. DeGraw's class. All of the walls in Ms. DeGraw's class are decorated with her students' work. On the north wall is a world map adorned with a drawing of each student's face and a piece of yarn connecting each student's face with the corresponding country he/she has come from. Also on the north wall is a poster board that is covered with handmade books about each student. These books contain a photograph of each student and is entitled "A Book About Me: My Whole Name Is…". Ms. DeGraw also goes to great lengths to use and affirm the diverse languages her students speak. Ms. DeGraw majored in French as an undergraduate; she often speaks in French with her students who are from Sudan and Congo, who are fluent in French. Ms. DeGraw has also managed to learn Spanish from her students, which she frequently uses to communicate with her Latinx students. In appreciation for learning languages, Ms. DeGraw had her students label every object in the class with index cards that not only have the English word for the labeled object, but also the name of the object in all the other languages the students speak.

The organization of Ms. DeGraw's classroom consists of seven tables, each occupied by three or four students. In the back of the room, there is a couch and a rocking chair where students can sit and read in a comfortable, home-like atmosphere. Here, students find bookshelves filled with books written in English as well as books written in the languages that are represented in the class. Ms. DeGraw's classroom is neat and tidy. All of the school supplies are put away in cabinets and there is very little paper work in her class, because Ms. DeGraw keeps all of her grading records and assignments on her computer. In the upcoming sections of this chapter, I discuss some of the multicultural practices that emerge in Ms. DeGraw's classroom as she attempts to advocate for her ESL students.

Inclusive Assignments

While the larger school goes to great lengths to silence and make the ESL student population invisible, Ms. DeGraw goes to great lengths to bring visibility to her students' linguistic, cultural, racial, immigration, and overall life experiences. Needless to say, the ESL students are very different from their White, English monolingual peers at DMS. Not only do they speak non-English languages and live culturally different lifestyles than their White, English monolingual peers, but also most of the ESL students are refugees from war-torn countries or from economically underdeveloped countries where their families were provided few to no opportunities for substantial employment. As a result of these circumstances, most of the ESL students have lived tough lives. Even though they are only 12–13 years old, their life experiences have already included experiences with death, bloodshed, hunger, unemployment, loss of loved ones, and separation from close family members, including sometimes parents and siblings. Even now that they are in the United States, many of the ESL students and their families are in survival mode, meaning they now live in a country where they do not know the language or culture, they struggle to find employment that recognizes their qualifications and abilities and that provides them a minimal means of living, and they are isolated from family members and support networks who have been left behind in their countries of origin. The life experiences that the ESL students bring with them to DMS are quite different from the life experiences of the White, English monolingual students who have lived their entire lives in the U.S., speak the dominant language, live economically stable lives, and have been socialized to be academically successful in a schooling context that exclusively promotes their culture and language. Despite the very different lifestyles that ESL students and White, English monolingual students at DMS experience, the ideology of invisibility at DMS deemphasizes this diversity and instead treats ESL students' salient cultural, linguistic, economic, religious, and immigration experiences as if they do not exist, and in effect, rendering them invisible.

In an interview Ms. DeGraw talks about her intentions to include her students' life experiences in the curriculum she delivers:

Ms. DeGraw: Well, I just, I try real hard to be inclusive. I try really hard to, um, emphasize the importance of students' voices. I try really hard to get, to let them understand that at least in my classroom, their cultures and their languages are really respected and coddled and nurtured and I, I love to learn their languages. I mean, they have equal importance with English.

In one way, the absence of a curriculum for ESL students reinforces their invisibility within the school and district contexts, but in another way it opens up the possibilities of what can be taught. Recognizing this opening for possibilities, Ms. DeGraw uses this opportunity to bring visibility to her students. Among the many inclusive assignments I observed in Ms. DeGraw's class is the "Class Mural and Story".

Class mural and story.   The "Class Mural and Story" assignment begins with students drawing a picture that represents their native country and/or culture. Ms. DeGraw explains to the class that the mural can include drawings of things that exist in their country, such as the people, cities, schools, vehicles, animals, cultural symbols, traditions, flags, soldiers, wars, etc. Each student begins by drawing his or her piece of the class mural with pencil on a piece of butcher paper that was once as large as the length of a classroom wall and has been cut up into 24 puzzle-like pieces, which represent the number of students who are in the class. Each student draws on a piece of paper that is roughly 11x12 inches in size. These pieces will all be taped together when students are done to create a class mural. After the students finish drawing their piece of the mural with a pencil, they then paint their pictures with vibrant colors.

In my field observations of the students doing this part of the assignment, I noticed that students drew pictures of their country's flags or religious symbols such as the cross, the Virgin Guadalupe, Jesus, angels, and churches. Students also drew pictures of parties and celebrations such as birthday parties and Las Posadas (A ten-day festival that centers on reenactments of the biblical Mary and Joseph trying to find lodging). Other students drew pictures of war. These pictures featured drawings of guns, soldiers, cannons, dead people, blown up houses and other buildings, blood, and helicopters.

The second part of the "Class Mural and Story" assignment required students to write a paragraph that describes what they have drawn. The students first write the paragraph in their native language. When they are happy with the content of the paragraph in their native languages, the students then translate the paragraph into English, using a variety of resources for translation, including their peers, digital translators, cellular phones, and print dictionaries. Students then type their paragraphs on the class computer and begin to go through an extensive revision and editing process that involves peer reviews as well as Ms. DeGraw reading and providing feedback on the paragraphs. Some of the stories that students attached to their drawings are as follows:

> This picture is about Bosnia. In this picture you can see soldiers. They are Bosnian soldiers. The name of this group is Zlatni Ljijani. They are very strong and honest. The name of this city is Tuzla. I grew up in Tuzla. During the war, I saw many people get shot.

> My picture is about the day of the workers. Mexicans have fiestas on this day. Those fiestas are only for poor people and for people that work really hard, not for rich people. The fiestas make people proud to be Mexican. On the day of the worker, there are many kinds of food—like tortillas with chile and juice. Mexican people share their food with poor people who don't have food.

> These are the soldiers in Sudan. The people from southern Sudan want to take things from the north, like cows and other animals, and the water that we drink. The guns that the soldiers use to fight also come from the north. My father was in the war in Sudan. He was fighting for the north.

These stories, along with all the others, were attached to the class mural. In addition to the polished English paragraph, students also attached the early version of their paragraphs that were written in their native languages. The finished product measures 25 feet by 5 feet, which Ms. DeGraw hangs in the school's front hallway, which is located at the entryway to the school.

The class time to develop the drawings and corresponding essays as well as the prominence of the final product at the entry of the school, no doubt brings visibility to the ESL students at DMS. It is unclear however what effect this visibility has in terms of transforming the larger sociopolitical context at DMS, which aims to silence and make these students invisible. In all actuality, Ms. DeGraw's attempt to bring visibility to her students may in fact do the opposite. In this assimilationist schooling context, the ESL students' narratives and drawings may signal to the larger school that the ESL students are still "other", not yet ready to participate in mainstream activities and classes. In addition to the non-English version of their essays possibly signaling "otherness", the presentation of their writing in their native languages, especially when compared to the accompanied English version of the paragraph, is underdeveloped and much less aesthetically appealing. Whereas the English language paragraph is well-developed, typed, and has gone through a rigorous revision and editing process, the native-language versions of the paragraphs are hand-written, underdeveloped, and in some cases, contain crossed out words and sentences. In other cases, the native language essays contain hard-to-read letters/words because they have been erased and then rewritten, sometimes a number of times. Portions of their native language writing appear on greyish, eraser-rubbed composition paper that is torn and raveled at the edges. While the class mural and story is certainly inclusive in that it makes ESL students' lived experiences, which are otherwise invisible at

DMS, visible, it may also reinforce the idea that English is the more elite, academic language—A language that is worthy of the revision process, word processing, and presentation in a more aesthetically appealing format than the paragraphs that students wrote in their native languages. Given that the students' native language is used to represent the students' roughest, unrefined version of their essays and the English language version represents the final, refined version, the two languages take on a continuum of progression, reinforcing the language hierarchy that is so prominent in our society—a hierarchy that positions standard English as the pinnacle of academic and professional communication. Thus, for this assignment, Ms. DeGraw may simultaneously challenge the ideology of invisibility while also reinforcing the prestige of the English language over the other languages her students speak.

Stereotype activity.   The class mural is an inclusive assignment because it showcases students' experiences that are otherwise silenced at DMS. The stereotype activity shares similar inclusive qualities in that it draws out and includes ESL students' oppressive experiences in the U.S. Ms. DeGraw considers this to be a consciousness-raising activity, because she wants her ESL students to be aware of the significance of the discriminatory remarks they receive as well as understand the concept of cross-group discrimination that her students experience. For the stereotype activity, Ms. DeGraw asks her students to move the tables to both sides of the classroom and for her students to form one big circle in the middle of the classroom. She then has the students sit on the floor and goes around to each student, handing them a business-sized envelope. Once every student has an envelope, Ms. DeGraw finds a space within the circle of students and sits down with them. Ms. DeGraw then addresses the class:

Ms. DeGraw: OK, I want you to open your envelopes and read what is inside.

The students open their envelopes and take a minute to read a message that is typed on a slip of paper. Ms. DeGraw then asks the students to go around the group and take turns reading their message out loud to the rest of the class. Many of the students, when doing this activity, speak very softly and have difficulty pronouncing the words. So for most students, Ms. DeGraw asks them to read the message as best they can and then Ms. DeGraw repeats the message to the group. For example a Mexican male slowly reads:

Emory: I don understan you. Espic English.

Ms. DeGraw then repeats the message by saying:

Ms. DeGraw: I don't understand you. Speak English.

The students continue to read the statements on their slips of paper in this fashion until all of the students have completed the task. Some of the messages that students read include the following:

Blacks should go back to Africa.

You White pig.

You are poor.

Indians are lazy.

You dirty Mexican.

Blondes are dumb.

That's so gay.

Hey nigger.

You fag.

You act like a girl.

Once all of the students have completed the task of reading their statements, Ms. DeGraw then goes around and asks the class to read their statement again, but this time stopping each time to discuss the meaning of each statement and asking students to share their own experiences with the statement. At this point in the activity, Ms. DeGraw passes out an index card to students which includes a list of words they can use to describe their feelings, such as: hurt, lonely, embarrassed, rejected. These words are printed in both English and Spanish and are used to help students express how they or others feel when they hear these statements. Some of the discussion that occurs during the course of this activity is as follows:

Diego reads his statement: You dirty Mexican.

Ms. DeGraw: Raise your hand if you're Mexican.

About half the class raises their hands. Edwin excitedly raises his hand as high as he can and then screams out "yeah!" to express his pride in being Mexican. Then another Mexican male, Isaac, joins the discussion:

Isaac:	I am not dirty!
Ms. DeGraw:	How does that make you feel if someone calls you a dirty Mexican?
Isaac:	Sad, hate, rechazado [rejected].
Ms. DeGraw:	It doesn't feel good. OK, next one.

Then a Chinese male reads his card:	You talk funny.
Ms. DeGraw addresses the whole class:	Do you speak English perfectly?

Students in unison:	Nooo!
Ms. DeGraw:	Does anyone ever make fun of you when you can't speak English?
Most students in class:	Yeah.

Ms. DeGraw: How does that make you feel?

Briana (Female Mexican Student): It makes me want to cry.

Ms. DeGraw: Some of you don't speak English very well. Is that OK?

Students in unison: Yeah.

Ms. DeGraw: Yes!!! You speak Spanish, Vietnamese, Bosnian. If you hear someone say, "Hey, speak English. You're in America," say "Hey, I speak Bosnian. I'm learning English". And that's OK. OK let's move on to another one.

Ms. DeGraw reads the next statement.

Ms. DeGraw: Hey nigger. Who knows what that means?

Only two students in the class raise their hands and both are Black males. Ms. DeGraw responds to the boys:

Ms. DeGraw: How does that make you feel?

Masakin: Sad.

Ms. DeGraw to class: Who do we say this to?

Masakin: To Black people.

Ms. DeGraw: To Black people. That word is used in this country and it used to be used a lot more. Remember Martin Luther King? Remember we talked about him? He said that it's not OK to use that word. It's racist. Does everyone know what that means, racist? Has anyone ever been called this [nigger]?

Masakin: Many times.

Ms. DeGraw: How did it make you feel?

Masakin: It made me feel very sad.

Rishi (male student from Congo): On the bus, they call me chocolate.

Ms. DeGraw: Is that a nice thing to say? Some people believe that if you have dark skin you are not OK. We're talking about prejudice.

In many ways, this class activity is an inclusive pedagogical practice because it invites students to talk about their personal experiences with these statements, but it is also a consciousness raising activity in that Ms. DeGraw tries to make the students across racial/ethnic/linguistic groups aware of what these statements mean as well as appropriate ways to respond to these statements. Ms. DeGraw tries to bring awareness to her students by asking them questions that prompt them to think critically about each of these statements. When discussing the statement, "Hey nigger," for example, Ms. DeGraw asks her students, "Who do we say this to?" With this question, Ms. DeGraw wants to make it clear to her students that people do not just use this word as a generic insult, such as could be the case with "hey, stupid". She wants her students to know that people use this term to specifically put down Black people and that it is racist. She also asks the questions, "Who has been called this?" and "How does it make you feel?" By asking "Who has been called this?", students can see who in class is the target of a specific statement. For example, when Ms. DeGraw asks, "Does anyone ever make fun of you when you can't speak English," almost every student responds affirmatively. By seeing others respond affirmatively, students can realize that statements like "You talk funny" are targeted towards ESL students across ethnic and racial groups, and again are not random statements that would be directed to just any person. In effect, Ms. DeGraw wants to draw attention to how ESL students are treated in this school and in the larger society.

In addition to Ms. DeGraw's attempts to make her students aware of the ways they are marginalized by these statements, she tries to provide them ways to respond to these statements. For example she states, "If you hear someone say, 'Hey speak English. You're in America,' say, 'Hey, I speak Bosnian [among other languages]. I'm learning English". By providing this response as an option for students to say, she encourages her students to reframe the negative message that points out what they do not know by highlighting what they do know and that they are in the process of learning English. This activity clearly counters the ideology of invisibility that circulates at DMS that renders invisible—among many things—ESL students' experiences with racism. Ms. DeGraw realizes that sustained incidents of racism, in addition to ignoring that they happen, negatively affect her ESL students.

As is the case with the other data I have highlighted so far in this book, there is complexity in the outcomes of this inclusive activity as well. While Ms. DeGraw may be successful at addressing some of the racial incidents some of her students have been a target of, she is unsuccessful in addressing the heterosexism that she, and possibly others in her class, endure. In the data that follow I discuss the stereotype activity further, demonstrating how the ideology of heteronormativity guides the discussion. One of the statements Ms. DeGraw included in the stereotype activity is: "That's so gay". Upon hearing this statement, many of the students begin to laugh.

Ms. DeGraw:	How do you say gay in Spanish?
Edwin:	Hoto
Ms. DeGraw:	Are there gay people in the world?
Students in unison:	Yes.
Ms. DeGraw:	Do you think they try to be gay?
A few students:	No.
Ms. DeGraw:	Is it wrong to be gay?
Edwin:	Yes.
Ms. DeGraw:	Is it their fault?
Edwin:	Because it's supposed to be a man and a woman not a man and a man.

Ms. DeGraw:	Well I think it's fine. OK, about 10%, diez por ciento son gay, OK. About one in 10 people are gay. OK how many people do we have in this classroom?

Students count and then respond: 25

Ms. DeGraw:	OK, about 25 and 1 in every 10 is gay. That means there could be 2.5 people in here that are gay.

Ms. DeGraw looks around the room for some type of response.

Ms. DeGraw:	OK, is it bad to be gay?
Edwin:	Yes.
Ms. DeGraw:	Is it bad to be Black?
Students:	No.
Ms. DeGraw:	Is it bad to be Mexican?
Students:	No.
Ms. DeGraw:	Is it bad to be blonde and to have blue eyes?
Students:	No.
Ms. DeGraw:	OK, is it bad to be gay?

Almost all the males in the class respond in unison: Yes.

Ms. DeGraw:	Why is it bad to be gay?
Masala:	Because they do bad things.
Ms. DeGraw:	Do straight people do bad things? Do Black people do bad things? Do Mexican people do bad things? No!

Ms. DeGraw points to a Mexican male in class and says:

Ms. DeGraw:	You're Mexican. I think that's good. I'm glad you're Mexican. That's who you are. We're talking about judging people.

Ms. DeGraw asks Edwin: Do you know this person [referring to the gay person he is vocally against]?

Edwin:	No.
Ms. DeGraw:	Is it OK to say a gay person is bad?
Edwin:	Yes.

Ms. DeGraw gets frustrated. She raises her hand, palm up, and asks: Why?

Edwin:	Because he's with a gay guy.
Masakin:	I saw a movie where it was wrong.
Ms. DeGraw:	And men and women don't do bad things?
Masakin:	No.
Ms. DeGraw:	What if I say I don't like you cause you're Black or African. Is that OK?
Masakin:	No.

Throughout the course of this activity, students have voiced their feelings and what it means to them when they are the targets of derogative statements. Suddenly, the activity takes a turn in a way that stifles Ms. DeGraw's voice and reinforces her invisibility as a lesbian. While she talks around the issue, she is careful to not include her own experiences as part of this discussion. Not knowing that Ms. DeGraw is lesbian and her own experiences with oppression, the students simply manufacture the heteronormative ideologies they have been exposed to in media and their everyday social experiences. The ideology of heteronormativity shapes the course of the discussion in such a way that Ms. DeGraw cannot penetrate the dominant way of knowing on this topic. On several occasions, Ms. DeGraw tries to offer alternative ways of thinking about gays and lesbians. She does this by trying to equate a gay/lesbian identity with a racial/ethnic identity, such as when she asks her students, "Is it bad to be Black? "Is it bad to be Mexican?" and then in her attempt to make a parallel, she asks, "Is it bad to be gay?" She also tries to penetrate the logic of heteronormative ideology by getting students to identify what it is that gay people do wrong. Assuming that her students think that the only bad thing gay people do is have sexual relations with each other, Ms. DeGraw then asks, "Do straight people do bad things? Do Black people do bad things?, and "Do Mexican people do bad things?" Ms. DeGraw is unsuccessful at making the point that people across races, genders, and sexual orientations engage in sexual relations, so gay people should be no different. From this activity, we can see that despite Ms. DeGraw's several attempts, she was unsuccessful at penetrating the powerful narrative of heteronormativity. In the following section, I discuss another inclusive project—the school video. Unlike what I have discussed so far, this project involves the White, English monolingual students who are enrolled in her elective video recording class.

School video. Ms. DeGraw's eighth-grade elective course is a video recording class, in which she teaches an all-White, English monolingual student population. One of the major projects in this class is the production of a "school video" that will be shown in new student orientations this upcoming spring. On the days I observed Ms. DeGraw's eighth period, the class was in the process of generating interview questions and were video recording the interviews they conducted with various students attending DMS. Even though the video recording class consists of all White, English monolingual students, Ms. DeGraw does not stray from her goals to bring visibility to the ESL student population at DMS. Thus, even when ESL students are physically absent from her class, Ms. DeGraw attempts to incorporate them as part of the class by drawing attention to their experiences at DMS.

In one of the video recording class sessions, Ms. DeGraw talks to her White, English monolingual students about the ESL population at DMS, explaining that many ESL students are not included in school activities and social groups. Later on in the period, Ms. DeGraw has the students work in groups, as they generate interview questions for the school video. In an effort to avoid the continued invisibility of ESL students, Ms. DeGraw talks to her eighth-period students and tells them that it is mandatory that they include ESL students in the school video, and further, that they should write some separate interview questions that specifically address the issues ESL students face at this school. Ms. DeGraw explains to the students that these interviews will be helpful to new ESL students who will be seeing the video, as they will learn a little bit about what to expect at DMS. Ms. DeGraw visits each table of students helping them generate interview questions for the ESL students they will interview. After a few days of revision and feedback from Ms. DeGraw, the interview questions they decided to ask ESL students include the following: Where are you from? Do you like DMS? Who is your favorite teacher and class? Have you been treated fairly and nicely at this school? Has anyone ever made fun of you because you don't speak English well or because you are from a different country? What advice would you give to an incoming ESL student? Do you like the ESL program and what do you like best about it?

In the making of the school video, Ms. DeGraw breaks from the ideology of invisibility by (1) informing White, English monolingual students about the experiences ESL students at DMS, and (2) inviting ESL students to speak about their experiences so that the school at large, and especially incoming ESL students, can be informed about the specific issues that are relevant to ESL students. However, despite Ms. DeGraw's effort to position ESL students prominently in the video by bringing visibility to unique circumstances, those ESL students who were interviewed for the school video did not take the opportunity to talk about their experiences. In comparison to the White, English monolingual students interviewed, who were loud, animated, and could not stop talking, the ESL students were quiet, reserved, and answered the interview questions with either a "yes," "no," or a quick one- to two-word response.

Further, the ESL students who were interviewed denied being treated unfairly or being made fun of at DMS. Only one Bosnian student said she was sometimes made fun of because she is an ESL student. Interestingly, these students were silent about these issues despite being very vocal in Ms. DeGraw's class about being mistreated as a result of their language, race, and newcomer status. Indeed, these were the same students who came to Ms. DeGraw with complaints about racism that occurs in their other classes, to which Ms. DeGraw addressed individually with accused teachers. In sum, despite Ms. DeGraw's attempts to make ESL students and their experiences at DMS visible to the larger school and incoming ESL students, for the most part, the ESL students reinforced their invisibility. In the end, ESL students' appearances and responses in the school video were brief. Despite Ms. DeGraw's best intentions to do otherwise, White, English monolingual students were the forefront of the majority of the video and the video overall failed to bring attention to the oppressive nature of DMS for ESL students.

Self-evaluations. At the end of each nine-week quarter, Ms. DeGraw has her ESL students fill out a form she calls "self-evaluation". She uses this form to assess how her students are doing and to receive feedback from her students on how the class is going for them. When I reviewed these self-evaluation sheets as part of my data collection, I took note of the questions Ms. DeGraw included on the evaluation sheet as well as the student responses. In reviewing the student responses, I found that despite the inclusive assignments and activities that drive Ms. DeGraw's ESL class, the students did not mention these assignments, much less an evaluation of them or a request for more of them. Instead of identifying and evaluating her multicultural approaches to teaching, the ESL students echoed the school districts' sentiments about the purpose of ESL classes: Learn English. After reviewing all of the students' responses, I found that their responses exclusively expressed their desire to learn English. The questions and some of the responses follow:

1. Do you like this class and why?
   - Yes, because I now lern more about English.
   - Yes, in class of Miss Ms. DeGraw I learn more English than other class.
   - Yes because is good for me for speak English. Yes, eseñan ingles y aprendo much [they teach english and I learn a lot].
2. Tell Ms. DeGraw something that she doesn't know about you.
   - Ms. DeGraw wy I can't go to level 2?
   - I want to go to level 2?
3. Tell me some things that you want to learn in the last 9 weeks of this class?
   - Speak Ingles [English] in the class with other person.
   - I wnt speak more English because I cant speak very well.
   - I want to go to level 2.
   - I want to lean about words past and everything you can talk for me. I hope you will for me about the word English in the last 9 weeks.

I was discouraged and surprised that the student responses never identified Ms. DeGraw's efforts to challenge the assimilationist context at DMS by bringing visibility to the students' cultural, racial, linguistic, and immigration experiences. Rather, their comments seemingly reinforced the assimilationist mentality of the larger school, by expressing that the only way they could gain visibility and credibility within DMS was to learn more English. Even in the second question wherein Ms. DeGraw seeks to learn more about her students in general, the students keep their responses centered on their desire to learn English, move on to ESL 2, which is one step closer to their integration with the White, English monolingual students in mainstream English-instructed classes.

It was almost the end of the school year and I had observed several times over Ms. DeGraw's attempts to disrupt the ideology of invisibility by including her students' cultural, linguistic, and racial experiences in the classroom and larger school. As I have reviewed in this case study, Ms. DeGraw went to great lengths to be inclusive as she often discussed their experiences with racism and linguicism, provided opportunities for students to talk and write about their cultural, linguistic, and immigration backgrounds, and allowing them to speak, read, and write in their own languages. Ms. DeGraw also put a strong effort into including students' languages in class activities and discussions. Despite working in an ESL program, which emphasizes English only, Ms. DeGraw often addressed the class in either Spanish so that her Latinx students could understand her or in French so that her African students could understand her. She also encouraged students to speak in their own languages in class and often promoted a mentality of learning languages as she often asked students to translate words or phrases from English to one of their primary languages so that she and the students can learn each other's languages. Indeed, Ms. DeGraw herself learned most of her Spanish, which she uses frequently, from students in her classes. Students were also provided many opportunities for reading books in their languages, as well as writing essays and doing homework assignments in their languages. These pedagogical practices both encouraged a learning environment where learning languages was considered positive and allowed students to continue to develop their literacy skills in their native languages while in the process of learning English.

Despite Ms. DeGraw's multicultural and multilingual efforts, the sociopolitical context at DMS and the larger society, which emphasized the importance of learning English, and English only, was too powerful to transform on a large scale basis. Students realized that in this country they and their families cannot advance academically or survive financially unless they are fluent in English. While their native cultures and languages may be important facets of their being, at DMS and within the larger society, their cultural and linguistic qualities are treated as a nuisance and a barrier and thus are to be made invisible. In the end, the students' comments reflect this reality of the school and social context, which tells them to discard everything that is not Eurocentric. Given this specific sociopolitical context, it is unclear what impact Ms. DeGraw's multicultural practices had in transforming the assimilationist ideology of the school or the schooling experiences of her ESL students in the larger school context.

CONCLUDING REMARKS

My aim in this chapter has been to demonstrate that Ms. DeGraw cannot be understood as being or not being an activist for her students or as implementing or not implementing multicultural education. This "either/or" framework that is so often utilized to understand teachers' multicultural work cannot account for the varied experiences that Ms. DeGraw underwent in her attempts to implement a multicultural education in her classes at DMS during the course of my study. It would be misguided advice to suggest that Ms. DeGraw needs to work harder or be more committed to the project of multicultural education in order to achieve a more desirable multicultural status or outcome. The reality is, Ms. DeGraw is embedded in a terrain of racial ideologies that produce ESL students as criminals and nuisances, and as such, are thought to be better off when they are made invisible. As argued in this chapter, even in Ms. DeGraw's many successes of interrupting racial ideologies through her inclusive assignments and by addressing racial injustices with White,

English monolingual students and teachers, the possibilities of achieving an idyllic notion of multiculturalism is nonetheless constrained. Based on this case study, Ms. DeGraw's multicultural practices in all of her classes, including her all-White, English monolingual video recording class, can be conceptualized in terms of both possibilities and impossibilities.

CHAPTER 4

MEGAN'S SCHOOL SUCCESS CLASS

It is just after lunch at Esplanade—an alternative high school and adult learning center. Many students at Esplanade eat lunch in their classrooms instead of the cafeteria, so several students are finishing their lunch in Megan's class and beginning to clean up as they throw away their empty Dr. Pepper cans, finish their last few nacho cheese fries, and pack away half-eaten bags of chips to save for later. Most students enrolled in Megan's School Success class spend their lunch period gathered around the several computers that are lined up on the east wall of Megan's classroom. As they eat their lunch, students listen to streaming music and browse the Internet. As the lunch hour comes to an end, Megan announces that it is time for class to begin and waits for the few students who did not spend their lunch period in her classroom to arrive. Once the students have a seat at the tables in her class, Megan begins teaching her School Success class. She grabs the students' attention by standing in the middle of the room and holding up a can of food with no label on it. In a loud, direct voice, she asks the class:

Megan:	What's in this can?
Lupe:	Peaches?
Kevin:	String Beans?
Megan:	Maybe. Do we know for sure? Usually cans of food have labels on them so we know what is inside. Do people have labels? Is there such a thing as a label free person?
Several Students:	No!
Megan:	No. They would be perfect to me, and that's impossible. Today I want everyone to write down and then share what labels are placed on them. I will start off by sharing how I think other people label me. People label me as a teacher, as power hungry, mean, as someone who doesn't listen, that I don't earn enough money for the work I do, that I have a dead end job, that I am not worth listening to as a person, a goodie-goodie, happy, talkative, pushy, racist because I am White. I really struggle with this issue of racism. I used to think I wasn't racist. Now I know I am. I used to think that all Native Americans are like "this". This didn't change until I came here [Esplanade]. At times I have gone to the store and only said hi to the ethnic people in the store so that they realize that I am not racist. But then I realized that

	I was not only labeling myself but also the people I was saying hi to, because I assumed they thought I was racist because I am White. I don't know. I really struggle with this. I am also labeled as rich, uncaring about the world, that I have a nice car, granola, tree hugger—depending on what I wear, that I am from a ranch, that I am always right, cocky, stuck up, popular, smart, non-tolerant, and perfect. Are all these labels true?
Students:	No.
Enrique:	Are any of them true?
Megan:	Well some are true.
Enrique:	How about being racist?
Megan:	I don't think I am anymore.
Enrique:	So you were? Wow! I didn't know that about you [Enrique shakes his head back and forth in disbelief and then looks down at the table in front of him].
Megan:	I say that, because I used to have the same expectations of all students from a particular group. For example, I used to think that all Polynesians were the same.

In this particular lesson in Megan's School Success class, she addresses the topics of labels and stereotypes. As the lesson progresses, Megan asks students to identify the labels that are placed on them and Megan writes these terms on the white board. This process generates a long list of labels, some of which include lazy, thief, criminal, gangster, whore, fag, loser, alcoholic, drugee, unintelligent, and soon to be pregnant. After the students are done naming off these various labels, Megan emphasizes that there is a big difference between this list of labels and reality. She ends the lesson by opening the unlabeled can of food and revealing to the students that it is a can of corn. Megan explains the analogy she is trying to make between the unlabeled can of food and her students' lives. She tells them that people often think they know what a person is about, but when they get to know that person better, they find out that the person is much different than what they initially thought. She explains, "Just like this can of food, one can't make assumptions about people until we know who they are".

During this activity, Megan reveals as much, if not more, about herself and how she is viewed in society as do her students. As is evident in the labels Megan identifies that apply to herself, many of these labels are based on privilege. As we will soon see, Megan is unlike Mr. Potts and Ms. DeGraw who both have first-hand experiences with discrimination. Megan has rarely been the victim of discrimination or oppression in her life, so she is in the unique position among the case studies in this book of confronting social justice issues as a novice. So when Megan teaches her students about labels and stereotypes, as she does in the above activity, she is simultaneously grappling with these concepts herself for the first time. From her interactions with her students, Megan is learning how social constructs of identity, such as race, social class, gender and sexuality impact her students' as well as her own life experiences. As a result of her teaching experiences at Esplanade, Megan is coming to terms with and confronting issues of her own whiteness and privilege. As part of this process, she contemplates, and often through her teaching experiences, whether she is racist or not.

In the above class activity, we can see how Megan struggles to make sense of being a White person in what she now realizes is a racist society. She explains that when she goes to the store, she wants to let "ethnic" people know that not all White people are racists and hopes to distinguish herself from other "racist" Whites by saying hi to people of color. Yet, as Megan continues to talk to her students about this process, she admits that she is racist. In identifying the labels that are placed on her, she comments, "I used to think I wasn't racist. Now I know I am". Then, seconds later when a student asks her whether it is true that she is racist, she responds, "I don't think I am anymore"—an admission that is clearly disappointing to at least one of her students. This lesson, as well as the others I present in this case study, demonstrate the inconsistencies that characterize Megan's multicultural practices. Through her teaching experiences at Esplanade, it can be said that Megan is gaining "racial literacy"—the ability to understand, build a vocabulary, communicate, and negotiate the concept of race (Twine, 2010; DiAngelo, 2012).

While focusing on the themes of teaching and learning, this chapter examines the (im)possible multicultural practices Megan delivers in her School Success class at Esplanade. In analyzing Megan's multicultural practices, it becomes evident that multicultural education is a complex process of teaching and learning, rather than an idealized identity or status that she can ultimately achieve. In an effort to situate Megan's (im)possible multicultural practices, I first elaborate on who Megan is and the school in which she teaches: Esplanade.

MEGAN

As I mentioned in chapter one, Megan and her family are wealthy. Even as an adult, Megan is supported financially by her family to the extent that her paycheck from her teaching position goes untouched and straight into a savings account. Because Megan was raised in an all-white, upper-class, gated community, she and her family have had little to no contact—much less relationships—with poor people and/or people of color. From Megan's own admissions, she and her family have often unwittingly perpetuated ideologies of white superiority. Now that Megan works at Esplanade, she is questioning and attempting to transform ideologies of white superiority, though she struggles to reconcile the two worlds (home and school) she lives and works in. Megan is often at odds with her family members, many of whom are educators themselves, about her teaching position at Esplanade. Megan's family cannot understand why she would want to unnecessarily expose herself to the perceived danger and "inferiority" they associate with Esplanade students. Megan discusses these conflicts she has with her family members:

Megan: And my parents are like, "we've worked so hard to give you so many privileges. Don't waste them," you know. And my vision is, "I'm not. I'm taking advantage of them". And my sister, who can't even walk on the same side of the street as a Mexican, tells me "you're holding their hands too much. You're um, they don't need a relationship. They need a teacher. Well, no wonder that 70% of them are ethnic, you know, in this area. That's how many of impoverished people are ethnic minority". And all of my sisters and mom and grandma are educators. And my extended family is even worse. They are just so hard to deal with. Because when I first got a job here I was so excited about it, and I didn't know anything about Esplanade before I applied here. And I went to a family dinner and one of my uncles teaches for Shasta [a traditional White and affluent high school on the West side of town]. He's the AP English teacher for Shasta, or he was. He's retired now. I told him, "Guess what? I got a job at Esplanade". And he was like "I'll get you a job at Shasta. You do not want to teach there". And I was like, "What?" And he said, "You don't know? Those kids are so bad. They treat you like crap and there's no real learning that goes on there. It's more like babysitting". And from then on, every time I talk to him he says, "If you want a job at Shasta, I'll get you a job there immediately". And my aunt, who is also a teacher, when I told her that I was going to teach AP English here, she was like, "oh my gosh, Megan. That would be such a disaster. Don't even try it. Those kids have no skills. No knowledge. They don't have any discipline. You're not going to be able to make that work". And they're all worried that I'm going to get [physically] hurt. They always want to know who got into a fight or who has been raped.

Working from the ideology of White superiority, Megan's family sees inferiority in the students who attend Esplanade—a perceived underclass that they do not want Megan to associate with. This becomes evident in that Megan's family members believe that Esplanade students do not have the academic abilities that White affluent students have and that they are physically dangerous. Megan's uncle, for example, tries to protect her by offering her a position at a White, affluent high school within the school district. Despite her family's desires, Megan continues to work at Esplanade. Esplanade is Megan's first teaching position after receiving her teaching certification and she is currently in her third year of teaching. Megan explains that working at Esplanade has brought a whole new perspective to her life and that she has made changes in her life as a result of that perspective. Megan explains:

Megan: I think so differently now that I am at Esplanade. One of my students came to me and told me that she went home and found both of her parents dead. So when I went home that day and the fact that my husband hadn't cleaned the house did not seem like such a big deal, you know? I mean, so my simple problems seem to take a greater perspective so that I don't need to stress out over these stupid things so much, you know. I feel like I have so many benefits in my life that I almost feel like if I were to complain for one second, I would be the biggest jerk alive. I cannot ignore what is going on in my and my students' lives and how different they are. I can't go back to not knowing.

By working at Esplanade, Megan has had to confront the ideology of white superiority. The dramatically different life worlds that she and her students occupy are often difficult for Megan to make sense of. One of the ways in which Megan tries to come to terms with the privilege she has in comparison to her students is by limiting her use of money and material goods as well as downplaying any physical manifestations of her wealth. For example, Megan and her husband no longer live in the all-white, gated community where Megan's extended family lives. They now live in a moderate neighborhood compared to her parents and siblings. She tries not to buy unnecessary things and often takes public transportation to and from school instead of driving a car. She purposely tries to tone down the material aspects of her appearance by wearing inexpensive clothing, which on most days consists of jeans, a t-shirt, and sandals. Megan does not style or color her hair or have an expensive haircut. She does not manicure her nails; she wears no make-up or jewelry whatsoever; and does not have any other accessories (e.g., a hand bag or book bag) that would reflect her access to material goods.

ESPLANADE

Esplanade is an alternative high school that also houses many adult education programs, including English as a Second Language (ESL), young parent programs, applied technology, and directed studies (a program that allows students to study at home and at school in order to obtain their high school diploma or their General Education Degree (GED). Esplanade serves more than 9,000 students, including 1,800 high school students, 4,300 adults studying for high school diplomas; 3,600 people from 80 nations learning English, and 180 teenage parents. Of the students who attend the high school, 77% are students of color. Also worth noting is that 90% of the students who are referred to Esplanade from traditional high schools are students of color. This can be compared to the school district overall, where 59% of their enrollment is made up of students of color. Among Esplanade high school students, 89% qualify for free or reduced lunch, 28 percent are learning English as a second language, and 17% receive special education services.

Andy Peterson, the principal at Esplanade, explains that there are four types of high school students who attend Esplanade. There are those students who live alternative lifestyles (gay/lesbian youth, religious minorities, homeless students, young parents, and students who do not believe in the traditional family lifestyle that is emphasized at home and at school). There are students who act out (fight, yell, swear, destroy property, etc.) in traditional schools because they have not experienced school success (reading, writing, social inclusion). The third group consists of students who stopped attending traditional schools altogether, because they did not find they could be successful there. Lastly, the fourth group consists of those students who, by choice, have never attended a traditional high school.

In this diverse school context, Andy sets the tone for transformative, multicultural schooling practices. The transformative practices and policies at Esplanade resonate with Nieto and Bode's (2012) notion of multicultural education being pervasive. As Nieto & Bode explain, multicultural education is not a frill that can just be added on to existing programs, policies, and curriculum; nor is it an activity or special event that can be scheduled into what is already happening at a school. Rather, as Nieto and Bode explain, "A true multicultural approach is pervasive. It permeates everything: the school climate, physical environment, curriculum, and relationships among teachers and students and community" (p. 50).

Through my interviews with Megan and Andy, I found that the transformative practices at Esplanade center on the idea of building relationships and respect for students. In order to do this, Andy explains that they attempt to break down traditional forms of power, or what Andy refers to as a "caste system"—a power system that appears in most traditional schools whereby teachers are treated as an empowered group and students are treated as a subordinate group. The power relations at traditional high schools that Andy refers to—what Esplanade tries to counter—is worth examining here. At traditional high schools, power relations are often defined as repressive, and thus are characterized by any or all of the following characteristics: top down (administrators have power over teachers and teachers have power over students), singular (power is often centralized in a single entity, such as administration), and unidirectional (only those with power can exercise power over their subordinates). In the traditional high schools within the district, teachers and administrators often employ repressive forms of power in that they attempt to police and keep surveillance on students. Traditional high schools, in comparison to Esplanade, attempt to treat power as a commodity, as something that teachers can and should have and that students should be without. This top-down approach to power pushes students to conform to preconceived notions of what a student should be. As a result, when students challenge these notions of power by not following the rules, they often have to face the consequences of school discipline policies, which in many cases, can result in a referral to Esplanade.

As can be presumed by the number of students of color who are referred to Esplanade, students of color experience disproportionate implementation of school discipline policies within the school district. These findings, however, are not unique to this school district by any means. When we examine how students of color are treated in schools across the nation, we see that they are more likely to be targets of school discipline and zero tolerance policies and are suspended and expelled more often than their White peers. A national study of school discipline finds that more than 70 percent of all school-related arrests or referrals to law enforcement agencies involve either Hispanics or African Americans (Education Week, 2013). Further, African Americans are three times more likely to receive a suspension or expulsion than white students (Lewin, 2012). Due to the historical consistency of these findings, many educational scholars have brought light to the systematic exclusion of students of color in what have been termed the educational and prison pipelines. Yosso (2006) and Yosso and Solórzano (2006) bring attention to the Chicana/o educational pipeline, by providing statistics for how many Chicana/o students fall through/are pushed out of the educational pipeline. Other scholars have focused on the school to prison pipeline. Laura (2014), in analyzing her younger brother's trajectory to prison, makes it clear that while her brother's story may be unique, the school-to-prison pipeline is unfortunately a well-paved pathway for African Americans. Laura states that while African Americans make up about 15 percent of those below the age of 18, they "make up 14 % of all school dropouts, 26 % of all the youths arrested, 46% of those detained in juvenile jails, and 58% of all juveniles sent to adult prisons" (p. 15). In examining the literature on zero tolerance, school discipline, and special education, Laura concludes that these "policies are panoptic systems of surveillance, exercises of power used to continuously and purposely monitor poor youth and youth of color" (p. 21). For many students, their enrollment at Esplanade is the result of their expulsion and thus referral from traditional high schools. Clearly, students who are referred to Esplanade within this particular sociopolitical context are viewed as part of the school-to-prison pipeline as the larger social context, including the traditional high schools within the district, define these students as pathological and see their pathway to imprisonment as inevitable.

When students arrive to Esplanade, they find that the power relations they experienced elsewhere are redefined. Unlike repressive power relations, Esplanade closely models Foucault's (1981) notion of power, which can be described as diffuse and multidirectional (e.g., circulating through everyone and working bottom-up, top-down, horizontally and diagonally). At Esplanade, teachers and administrators attempt to counter repressive power relations by removing all markers of power. For example, all teachers and administrators are called by their first names; thus my reference to Megan and Andy is by their first names, not their last names. Further, there are no designated "faculty" spaces within the school. That is, there is no lounge, office space, lunchroom, parking spaces, or bathrooms that are designated for faculty. There are no desks in the school, as desks can serve as symbols of power, especially for the teacher who uses a desk to create separation between her/himself and her/his students. Perhaps without realizing it, the teacher who positions her/ his desk at the front of the classroom with all the students facing the teacher sets up a banking model of education—a disengaged form of education wherein the teacher unilaterally deposits information into students' minds (Freire, 2000). Instead of desks, Esplanade uses tables that can be put together for a conference-style classroom or separated for small group work. Further, students and teachers have equal access to all school equipment, including phones, copy machines, computers, printers, etc.

Traditional working roles and divisions of labor are also blurred at Esplanade. Students volunteer at the on-site, student-parent daycare, where students provide care for some of their classmates who have a child. Students are also involved in various beautification and maintenance projects that attend to the physical appearance of Esplanade: picking up litter, gardening, landscaping, and painting the school. Another alternative practice employed at Esplanade is that the rate of learning and achievement is self-monitored and determined by students. Students can turn in assignments when they feel they are ready, can take tests when they feel they are prepared, and they can continue to work on assignments and take tests until they are satisfied with the results. These testing and assignment policies are an attempt to alter the traditional power dynamic between teacher and student. Instead of the teacher dictating when tests and assignments are due and that grades are final at that point, students determine what is best for their learning experiences.

In addition to breaking down traditional symbols of power, teachers and administrators also put great effort into building relationships with their students. Andy states that there are four main reasons why Esplanade students do not experience success at traditional high schools, most of which indicate the lack of student-teacher relationships the students had at their previous schools. These reasons include: (1) identity (no one knows who they are; teachers do not know their names), (2) belongingness (being part of social groups), (3) safety, and (4) an inability to meet standard classroom criteria. The lack of caring and student-teacher relationships Andy refers to is consistent with Valenzuela's (1999) study, which shows that Latinx school failure and high school drop out rates are the result of the lack of care, especially from teachers. In their traditional high schools, the lack of student-teacher relationships communicates to students that they are not important enough to get to know and that they have nothing of value to contribute to their schooling experience. For these reasons, low income and students of color often feel disenfranchised from schools, often resulting in school failure or withdrawal from school altogether. Esplanade tries to transform these negative experiences and outcomes by creating opportunities for teachers and administrators to build relationships with their students. Impressively, Andy visits each and every high school classroom every day at Esplanade and knows nearly every student by name. As I have discussed, there are also many policies within Esplanade that facilitate student-teacher relationships. Some of these policies include: (1) everyone is called by their first names, regardless of status within school, (2) nearly all markers of status (separate faculty spaces) are eliminated, (3) teachers eat lunch with their students, (4) teachers greet students in the hallways by their names when they arrive to school and teachers walk students outside the building at the end of the day (much like they would to a friend or family member who was visiting their home).

Esplanade's curricular programs also focus on student-teacher relationships and school success. Two classes are specifically designed around the concept of teacher advocacy and school success. Students are required to attend an advisory class and a school success class. The advisory class is designed for teachers to advocate for a small group of students. The class contains roughly 15–20 students who meet everyday for 20 minutes. The advisory class has no designated curriculum except for teachers to personally connect and advocate for their students. Teachers use this time to get to know their students and become aware of any issues either inside or outside of school that may serve as barriers to students' school success. As part of the process of getting to know their advisory students, the teachers often get to know personal details about their students, including who their family members are. Megan describes her school advisory class in the following way:

Megan: We have about 15–20 students who are with us for their entire time at [Esplanade]. And um, we know about, we know about their family. We get to know their boss. We know where they work. We have been to their house. We, um, if they aren't in school we know why. We call them every time they're absent or they call us and leave a voicemail and what happens is if a student has a problem, like even a problem like "we're being evicted from our house", the parent sometimes will even call me and so it's like you're an advocate for them too, you know, and suddenly, you're helping the whole family to find a house to live in and you know all sorts of things.... But um, anyway so the student comes, if my student has a problem with a teacher, um he walks into a classroom and the teacher says, "yeah, glad you showed up" or something like that, and the students really feel terrible about it. They come to me and if they don't feel comfortable going directly to the teacher they come to me, and I walk up with them to the class and the student and I will talk about how they can say what they need to say, how they can communicate it, and then they'll walk in and talk to the teacher, and my job is to make sure the students are treated fairly, so I'm a mediator almost. But really I'm there for the student. So I think that makes them feel empowered.

Esplanade also requires their high school students to attend a school success class. The curriculum used in the school success classes, "Techniques for Tough Times," was developed at another local high school and focuses on students acquiring the skills they need to be successful in school even when they face difficult circumstances. As Megan explains, "this program seeks to have students feel connected to their school and to help them solve the problems behind their academic problems". Megan has 20 students in her school success class. Of these students, 8 are African American, 9 are Latinx, 2 are white, and 1 is Samoan.

The alternative practices that are employed at Esplanade seem to have a positive impact on student achievement. Andy explains how the practices at Esplanade, in comparison to traditional high schools within the school district, are reflected in Esplanade students' test scores:

Andy: We get the lowest two quartiles of students, and 90% of them are poor and ethnic minority, so there's something going on there [with placement]. We know that poor kids and ethnic minority kids do not test well, do not do well on standardized tests [at traditional high schools]. I believe because traditional schools don't teach these kids in the right way. In the math and language arts we [Esplanade] outperform [the other high schools in the district] by 9 percentage points in language arts and 8 percentage points in math. It's not the kids. These kids aren't being taught [in other schools]. There isn't an environment where they feel comfortable going.

Andy goes on to explain that Esplanade is the safest high school within the district. It has lower incidents of vandalism and violence than all the other high schools in the district. He is proud to point out that there has not been a fight at Esplanade for 3 years and the school walls are graffiti free. Even though most students regret having to go to Esplanade when they first receive a referral, most of the students decide to stay at Esplanade until they graduate, even when they are provided the opportunity to return to their traditional high schools.

SOCIOPOLITICAL CONTEXT

In order to understand the (im)possibilities of Megan's multicultural pedagogical practices, it is important to contextualize her work within a sociopolitical context which includes specific racial ideologies that define Megan's and her students' educational experiences. These racial ideologies include: White superiority, student pathology, and school success. As will be evidenced in the forthcoming examination of Megan's school success class, these ideologies merge together to inform complex pedagogical practices as Megan attempts to advocate for and deliver transformative pedagogical practices to her students.

To see how the ideologies of white superiority and student pathology work in tandem, we only need to look to the comments Megan's family members made about Esplanade students. While Megan's family members do not verbally identify race as part of their narratives, it is clear that race is the construct that guides their thinking. By stating that "We've worked so hard to give you so many privileges," Megan's family members recognize that she is privileged and that she is degrading herself as well as putting herself in physical danger by working at Esplanade. Her uncle even offers her a teaching position at the all-White high school within the school district, where she would presumably preserve her white superiority and not put herself in danger by being around the pathological students at Esplanade. The ideology of student pathology also surfaces in spaces located outside the school. Those who do not work at Esplanade, such as communities surrounding the school and those who are part of traditional high school settings often employ the ideology of student pathology when describing Esplanade students. For the most part, outsiders perceive

Esplanade as a dangerous place that is filled with society's rejects. Traditional high schools, for example, issue referrals to students who are "underachievers", students with truancy and discipline problems, and those who generally are unable to conform to the traditional high school setting. The ideology of student pathology also emerges in the practices of local community members. For example, when students visited a nearby antique store after school, the owner of the antique store wrote Andy a letter stating that Esplanade students are not welcome in the store. Part of this letter states: "Although I am sympathetic to the situations of your students, I cannot allow a group of juveniles with possible connections to gangs, drugs, and other illegal activities to browse through my store, especially with their teacher pointing out to them the large prices of the items located here". This letter essentially bars Esplanade students from the store and rationalizes this decision by employing the student pathology ideology. Megan addresses the ideology of student pathology in an interview:

Megan: When I tell people that I teach at Esplanade and that it's an alternative high school, everyone thinks that, "Oh my gosh. That must be so hard". And everybody wants to hear my horror stories. I mean, it's just the biggest deal ever. Um, and so everyone wants to hear me taking a knife away from a kid or um, they want to hear about some kid who told me to "fuck off" or something like that, you know, which happens every once in a while. That's true, but it, I think that they have this vision that it happens all the time. I think the other misconception that they have is that our school is, um, dirty and dark and um, you know, that the kids are sassy. I don't think that the larger society thinks that my kids want to learn. They think they're all just, you know, these thugs who are going to make nothing of their lives. And that our job is to keep them out of jail. When they think of Hispanics, they think of a particular image of a Mexican. A Mexican wearing gang clothing. And um, I mean I think there are tons of judgments—sexual promiscuity, you know, that their parents can't get a job or maybe once they start thinking sympathetically, maybe they think that all of them are beat up by their parents and that's why they are the way they are, which is true of some, you know, but that's always going to be true of some and not others.

Because the ideology of student pathology circulates in the surrounding local communities and traditional high schools, it invokes an image of Esplanade as an undesirable option for high school students in traditional high schools. According to this ideology, which is no doubt convincing, Esplanade students are seen as criminals, gang members, and troublemakers and Esplanade is no more than a holding cell that prolongs students' eventual incarceration.

In contrast to the ideologies of white superiority and student pathology, is the ideology of school success. By centering on the concept of school success, Esplanade is unlike Viewpoint Elementary and Drew Middle School—both of which defined their students of color in terms of deficits. At Esplanade, even though many outsiders may employ the ideology of student pathology to construct Esplanade students as dangerous, criminal, and unwilling to learn, those who work within the school believe that Esplanade students are successful students. Andy, Megan, and the overall teaching staff all emphasize that their students are successful at Esplanade. Taken together, these conflicting ideologies of white superiority, student pathology, and student success make up the sociopolitical context that Megan teaches in. Informed by these conflicting ideologies, and consistent with the theme of this book, Megan's pedagogical practices are contradictory in nature. That is, in her attempts to advocate for her students, she both challenges and reestablishes the racial status quo, thus embodying the (im)possible multicultural teaching disposition. In looking at the complexity of Megan's pedagogical practices, I start off by examining how Megan, at times, reestablishes traditional power relations by positioning herself as her students' savior.

TEACHER AS SAVIOR

Despite the school's and Megan's attempts to break down all power symbols that establish a hierarchy within Esplanade, Megan, at times, (re)establishes herself as morally superior to her students. Throughout the various school success activities Megan has her students participate in, which I will get to shortly, Megan teaches her students various strategies so they can take the moral high ground in dealing with the various problems they have in their lives. As Megan describes below, she sees this work as service work or charity, which she is privileged enough to deliver to this community of students. In the following discussion, we can see how the moral concept of savior emerges from experiences Megan has had at Esplanade as well as from the moral lessons she has been taught at her home and church.

Megan: My big thing was that I knew a lot of really great people [prior to working at Esplanade], you know, but they were great people who had everything in the world, and they were all helping each other, and that's what I thought people did. That's what I learned in my church. Help your neighbor. You know, I thought, this is what I'm going to be working in too. I'm going to be helping Kathy, who's my neighbor and her kids, you know, instead of thinking like I do now, that Kathy doesn't need my help. She's fine. And there are other people who need it, you know. And um, so like when I became a teacher I wanted to teach AP English, and I wanted to get in the best school. I wanted to be a teacher in the best school in the city, and I wanted to teach the highest level class. And now I'm saying to myself, "Wait a minute. Those kids in those classes are going to succeed no matter who their teacher is, and I want to help people who are not going to succeed unless they have the right teacher. And I'm going to be as flexible as I can until I'm the right teacher for each individual kid...". So, I mean, I think that's where really my goals have changed in terms of my career is that I no longer want to help people who I don't think need my help as much. I want to go where I'm needed the very most. But, I would say that in general in my life that, um, I think, I feel a greater responsibility to share what I have and what I know.... Cause what I see is that my students, they're just all learning from each other and none of them have any skills, so the things that they're learning are incorrect or are not going to make them happier people, you know. Um, so hoping not to sound prideful by saying that, I, I mean that's really how I think I've shifted. And um, I mean even to turn this even into a religious thing, I feel really strongly about, um, Jesus Christ, and um, be forgiving, and um, love the people who are not getting love, you know. And I thought I was doing that before. And now I'm realizing that I wasn't, and that there is a whole group of people out there who need my love, you know, and who need love in general, whether it's mine or anybody's. They don't care. They need some.

As can be seen in this interview, the concept of teacher as savior emerges from Megan's church, where it is emphasized that people must help their neighbors and those who are less fortunate. While well-intended, this savior orientation, along with the self-help activities emphasized in the school success curriculum, merge to position Megan as her students' savior and creates a pedagogical orientation that draws out her students' perceived problems that must be fixed. From Megan's statements, "I want to help people who are not going to succeed unless they have the right teacher," one can see that Megan's work at Esplanade fulfills a particular aspiration to do charity work.

Interestingly enough, Megan is not exclusively positioned as her students' enlightened savior. Of course, Megan's teaching disposition shows great complexity, and so it should not be surprising that in addition to being the enlightened savior, Megan also occupies the position of the humble learner. In the instances when Megan becomes the humble learner, Megan's students become her teachers, which is clearly an example of the transformative power relations that take place at Esplanade. In the following section, I focus on the ways in which Megan is a learner at Esplanade. However, even while Megan is positioned as the humble learner, her white superiority becomes front and center to these educational experiences.

MEGAN AS HUMBLE LEARNER

In stark contrast to Megan as the enlightened savior to her students' unfortunate lives is Megan as the humble learner. As explained earlier, even though Megan has always been a racial being who has benefited from her Whiteness, it has been only recently at Esplanade that she begins to consider the significance of her own and her students' race. Working at Esplanade has provided her the opportunity to come into contact with racial others for the first time in her life and to begin thinking about the personal and social implications of race. Megan talks with her students in her School Success class about her first experiences at Esplanade, when she believes she first encountered racial and social class differences:

> Megan: I think there is a misunderstanding between Hispanics and all other minorities. Like me, I grew up in an all White neighborhood, all WHITE [emphasis in tone]! The only Hispanic people I knew were the people who did our yard. I didn't talk to a Hispanic until I came here to Esplanade. When I first came here I taught adult ESL and I was like telling them [the students] that if they're making less than $8 an hour, then you're getting taken advantage of. I was telling them, "You're smart. You need to become a lawyer". And they were like, "We're glad to have the jobs we have. If White people don't want to do it [their jobs], we'll take those jobs they don't want". It was a total eye opener to me.

The relationships that Megan has formed with her students have served as the impetus for Megan to explore and struggle to understand the significance of social class and race.

One of Megan's central struggles is coming to terms with whether or not she is racist. In many ways, Megan realizes she is racist and she seeks to fully recognize the ways in which she is racist in her quest to not be a racist. While Megan does not consider herself a racist who explicitly espouses hateful comments or behaviors, she is concerned with the more subtle ways she may reinforce racist stereotypes. This learning process was apparent in the opening dialogue in this chapter when Megan talked to her students about her struggle to understand her role in a racist society. As she explained, she wants to communicate to people of color that she is not racist by saying hi to people of color she encounters in public spaces, but then she realizes that she may be reinforcing racial constructs by doing this. In the following interview excerpt, Megan discusses at length her struggle to come to terms with racism.

> Megan: I think it's a huge struggle. I think that it, I think it really has been all about communication for me. Um, I mean I have so many, you know like I was talking about bringing lemonade to the guys who were working on my yard. Well, I mean I think that I, I did that purposely to show I'm not racist, I'm not one of them. And I always have this inside of me. I'm not one of them. I mean I want people to know that, you know. And um, and it's terrible. I think I was always fearful that someone would think that I was racist. But, I don't think I realized that I was racist till I started talking to people about things that have happened to them, and realizing, "Oh my gosh". That would have easily been me. I could have said that.

I could have done that". And um, I mean like them talking about, my students talking about how often they get pulled over [by cops], and this isn't my high school students either. This is even my adult students, you know. And um, I was thinking about one time when I was driving home from California and I saw these, this cop pull over this Mexican couple, see, Hispanic, I don't know what they were. Um, Hispanic couple and I thought to myself, "There's probably drugs in their car". And so things like that are what I remember when my students are telling me comments they get, because I realize I think them. And so I've had a really hard time, um, I just think that so much of racism is subconscious, and I think what I've come to grips with is that I need to stop deciding that I'm racist and someone else isn't or that because I'm White I'm racist, or because I'm White I need to not be racist or whatever.

As indicated in this interview excerpt, as a result of the conversations Megan has with her students, she realizes that race has great significance not only in her students' lives, but in her own life as well. This is important, because many White teachers only see race as a construct that affects the lives of their students of color. On rare occasions will White teachers see how race affects White people, including themselves, or think of themselves as somehow being racist. As I discussed in chapter 1, some teachers do recognize teacher racism, but often not in themselves—but in the teaching practices of other teachers. This was the case in the teaching disposition of The Detached Teacher: A Case of Racist Teachers. Unlike the detached teacher, Megan is willing to realize and confront her own complicity in racism. In doing so, Megan draws from her students' experiences with race and racism as resources to learn about racism. Students' experiences with racism not only become evident to Megan in the school success activities that focus on race, but they also emerge in race-centered conversations Megan has with her students. Interested in understanding her own complicity in racism, Megan asks her students to inform her of the ways in which she may be racist towards them. In the following passage, Megan describes an incident when a student took the opportunity to tell her that she was being racist towards him.

Megan: And it's hard for me to tell my students that I'm not like that [racist], because in some ways I feel like I am and I'm trying to get over it, so I tell them that. I say, "Yes I do. I know I have some expectations that are different. You got to tell me when you see me treating you differently from someone else, so that I get better," you know. And when that comes out then, I mean, students do call me on it a lot. Like I had this one student last year, he was getting a 'C' in my class, and I said, "That's great. Fabulous job. You're going to get a 'C'.' And later on he came back and said, "You told me I was doing a fabulous job, because I got a 'C.' When you were in high school would you have accepted a 'C' out of yourself?" And I said, "No. I would have expected an 'A'.' And he said, "Well, why did you expect me, that I should get a 'C' and that's really great work for me? You know that I could get an 'A.' Why didn't you tell me that's not acceptable and that I needed to work harder and get an 'A'". And I was like, "I don't know". And he said, "Because I'm Hispanic. Because you thought it was really great that here I am Hispanic and I'm passing".

Megan appreciates these learning moments and thanks her students for identifying the ways in which they see her as racist. Being involved in this learning process with her students demonstrates how Megan is dedicated to the process of multicultural education and is genuinely interested in knowing what she can do in her life and in her teaching experiences to confront racism. In these instances, Megan turns the teacher as savior script on its head. As a humble learner, Megan realizes that her students are more knowledgeable than herself on the topics of race and racism and she has no problem transforming traditional teacher/student roles so that she can confront these difficult issues in her attempts to become a better person and teacher.

To complicate matters though, at the same time Megan's disposition as a humble learner disrupts traditional power relations between teacher and student, this particular disruption is not straightforward. While Megan is clearly disrupting traditional power relations when her students become her teacher, traditional power relations seem to be restored when Megan identifies herself as racist and asks her students to provide evidence of such. Even though Megan brings complexity to the concept of racism by recognizing the ways in which she is racist and not racist, her students seem to be working from a more concrete idea of racism. Based on her students' responses in these teaching/learning interactions, there seems to be no "in-between" when it comes to racism: You are either racist or you are not. Even someone who admits to being a little bit racist is deemed a racist in this context. Thus, when Megan admits to being a racist in her class and asks her students to point out the ways in which she is racist, she reestablishes the racial order that openly exposes her White superiority and privilege and her students as victims of her own racism. This becomes evident when Megan admits to being racist and students respond with shock, because they believed she was not a racist. Students' responses to Megan's pedagogical practice of stating she is a racist may actually distant herself from her students in that she becomes categorized as "one of them"—a racist instead of as an advocate for her students. Thus, in Megan's attempt to break down student/teacher power relations by creating moments when her students become teachers, these power relations are more than likely reestablished when Megan identifies herself as racist. Thus, in her attempts to join forces with her students by learning how she can become an anti-racist advocate, Megan reestablishes her racial privilege, and is ultimately another White person responsible for her students' marginalization.

These findings are evident in the opening of this chapter when Megan talks about the various labels people place on her. One of the labels she mentions during this conversation is that of being racist. A Mexican student asks her about this, and when Megan confirms it used to be true, the student responds by saying, "So you were? Wow! I didn't know that". The student then lowers and shakes his head back and forth in disbelief. Although I did not speak to this student, it seems as though his disappointment is rooted in the realization that Megan is racist. In this case, while Megan does achieve the goal of learning from her students, it may be at the cost of her students' learning experiences. It remains unclear as to what extent Megan hinders her students' learning experiences by openly discussing and struggling through her "racist/not racist" process.

To further elaborate on the (im)possibilities of Megan's pedagogical practices, I now turn to the specific activities Megan implements in her School Success class. Consistent with the theme of this book, Megan's advocacy for her students in her School Success class involves a process that is imbued by contradictions. Even though the ideology of school success shines a positive light on Esplanade students and serves as a counter narrative to the student pathology narrative, the school success curriculum and pedagogical practices in some ways reinstate problematic approaches to teaching that position students as the source of their problems and even undermines their agency.

SCHOOL SUCCESS CLASS

Megan's School Success class contains 20 students and meets everyday for 50 minutes during 5th period, which is right after lunch. The purpose of the school success class is for teachers to teach students how to advocate for themselves by providing them with various self-help strategies to work on issues concerning their self-esteem, relationships with others, and the overall oppression they endure as a result of their multifaceted identities, including social class, race, language, immigration background/status, gender, sexuality, etc.

Within the various class activities that make up the school success curriculum, there is a heavy emphasis on the concept of self-help, which pushes students to develop strategies to (1) identify the problems that stand in the way of their school success, and (2) develop problem-solving techniques they can use to overcome these problems. As we will see shortly, the self-help activities are imbued with multicultural contradictions when it comes to student agency. On the one hand, student agency is front and center as students solve their own problems in order to achieve academic success. On the other hand, these activities undermine student agency by positioning students as the culprits of their problems, and as such, pushes students to fix themselves, not the external ideological and institutional forces that give rise to any number of the larger social justice issues they face. I begin to unravel the contradictory nature of the school success curriculum and Megan's pedagogical practices by presenting a few of the school success activities, including the final exam for this class. I first present these activities and then I analyze the (im) possibilities of these activities as a whole. The first in-class activity is called: I'm Only Really Happy When I'm Miserable.

I'm Only Really Happy When I'm Miserable

The theme for today's School Success class is: "I'm Only Really Happy When I'm Miserable". This statement is written under the topic of the day, which is written on the white board under the heading "School Success". Megan gives the students a handout that begins with a quote by William Shakespeare, stating "Nothing is good or bad, but thinking makes it so". The handout goes on to state:

> The meaning of life's events lies in our perception or interpretation of them. How many times have you changed your mind about a teacher, coach, or event only after you know more about them? There is power in accepting things as they are, in not judging it to be good or bad until we see how things turn out. Many times we make ourselves miserable by looking at things as "awful". We can make ourselves miserable, unhappy and sick…. First we must become aware of what is not working. Then we can change our responses and experiment with creating a more positive outcome. REFRAMING. We need to take responsibility for the ways in which we make ourselves miserable. Obviously, if we can make ourselves miserable we can also take responsibility to act in ways that make ourselves happy and fulfilled. We can purposely do more to take care of ourselves.

As indicated in this handout, students are seen as responsible for their misery and likewise for acting in ways that make them feel "happy and fulfilled". As such, students are to learn that they alone determine how they feel and how they think, and if they can reframe their negative perceptions to positive ones, they can be successful in school and in life. After reading the handout to her students, Megan asks her students in a whole-class discussion:

Megan: What's something that's really bad that can happen to you?
Student: Get stranded.
Student: Get shot.
Megan: Ok, good. Do you think I would have a different perspective if I got shot?
Student: Yes. You would value your life more.
Megan: What would you value more?
Student: Life.
Student: Your body.
Student: Family.
Megan: Could you say that getting shot could actually make your life better?
Student: It's not the actual event that you would learn from, but what happens afterwards.

A few girls speak out, saying that they do not think anything good can come from being shot. Megan responds:

Megan: You don't think good experiences can come from any experiences?
Girls: No.
Megan: Like what kind of experiences can you not benefit from?
Female
Student: Getting raped.

A few other female students from across the room join the conversation. I cannot make out what they say, but a girl responds to Megan by saying:

Female
Student: You can't tell a guy to use protection before you get raped!

Not necessarily addressing this students' point, Megan continues to try to convince the students that something bad can turn into something good if they just change their perspectives.

The goal of this class activity is for students to take the worst problems they may have in their lives (e.g., getting shot) and begin to think about how these incidents can be viewed positively (e.g., having a new outlook on life). In this self-help activity, Megan pushes her students to think about how they may encourage misery in their lives. According to this perspective, students can take their worst problems and reframe them as something positive that has happened in their lives.

Reframing Personalities

Similar to the "I'm Only Really Happy When I'm Miserable" activity, which has students reframe tragic events they have experienced, the reframing personalities activity has students reframe the relationships they have with people that often impact their lives in a negative way. The school success curriculum posits that if students can individually reframe the negative personalities of others into positive ones, they will have better relationships with these people, thereby decreasing the problematic relationships they have with their friends and family members. It is reasoned that this process will ultimately contribute to the students' school success. Megan begins the "Reframing Personalities" lesson by explaining to the students what the class activity is for the day.

Megan: We are going to reframe negative comments that are listed on
           a worksheet that reflect certain personality types by writing a
           corresponding but more positive attribute.

In a whole-class activity, the students, along with Megan's help, reframe negative personality attributes into positive ones. Megan writes a list of negative attributes on the white board, which appear in the list below to the left. They then work to come up with the reframed positive attributes, which are listed below on the right.

1. "They think they are superior beings…"	Confident, take pride in themselves
2. Arrogant	Confident
3. Heartless	Can control emotions
4. Don't care about people	In control of emotions
5. Ruthless	Determined
6. Unrealistic	Imaginative
7. Eccentric or weird	Don't care what people think
8. Poor dresser	Don't care what people think
9. Emotionally controlled	Patient
10. Repressed	Patient/controlled
11. Rigid	Organized/ consistent
12. Controlling	Organized/ helpful
13. Dull or boring	Relaxed
14. Stubborn-pigheaded	Never gives up/confident
15. Opinionated	Confident
16. System-bound	Traditional
17. Unimaginative	Realistic
18. Uncreative	Realistic

After the class is done reframing the negative attributes into positive ones, Megan addresses the class:

Megan: Notice how you can take a negative or a put-down and change it into a positive. Think about that in terms of the people you know. When you think someone is being controlling, remember that they can also be seen as organized and helpful. Remember that in your relationships. I once had a pregnant student who did this exercise in my class and this exercise helped her to see that she and her mom had different personalities. She thought her mom hated her because of her pregnancy, but then she realized that they just handled the situation in different ways.

After this class session, Megan further explained to me the purpose of this activity.

Megan: This activity is to help the students in their relationships, the way they feel about the people in their lives. I want them to know that positive language changes a relationship.

This class activity, which focuses on relationships, asks students to think about how they can reframe what they perceive to be negative attributes in those people they have relationships with into positive ones. In this exercise, students are to take responsibility to help themselves create functional relationships in their lives. Depending on how they think, not on how others act, the relationship can be perceived positively or negatively.

Final Exam: Reframing for Power

The final exam in Megan's School Success class draws from the reframing activities such as those described above, by presenting a series of written scenarios that Megan's students often face in their home lives that come to impact their school achievement in a negative way. After reading each scenario, students are to use the "reframing" skills they have been learning all semester to rewrite the negative scenario into a positive one. As is the case with all the reframing curriculum, this exercise is to show students that when they reframe a negative situation into a positive one, they reposition themselves as having power in the situation. Their power in these scenarios lies in their ability to reframe how they perceive the situation. The following passage is one of the negative scenarios on the final exam that students have to rewrite/reframe into a positive version.

> My mom just lost her job because she drinks too much, and now we might be kicked out of our apartment. She never paid the rent anyway—just spent it on drinks. She is never around to help, and I feel total responsibility for my younger brothers and sisters. I always have to clean the house, and now my brothers are starting to get into trouble. I don't know if I should start taking over. My mom doesn't seem to care at all, so I think someone needs to get involved, but it's not my job. I shouldn't be the one to do it.

A few days after the final exam, Megan goes over the test scenarios with her class. When she discusses the above stated scenario, she explains to the class what she is looking for in their rewrites. As Megan explains to the class, a positive version of the story above might read as follows:

> My mom trusts me a lot. She allocates a lot of family responsibilities to me and believes I can do a good job. For example, I am often expected to clean the house and take care of my younger brothers and sisters. I understand that my mom can't handle the stress of working full time and taking care of us kids by herself. She often deals with the stress by drinking. I can understand the stress she experiences, because I am stressed with the responsibilities of school and family. I try to handle my stress effectively though by thinking positive and doing some relaxing activities such as riding my bike.

Students then compare this "model" response to their own responses on the final exam. After going over the entire exam, students review the grade they received on the exam and then decide whether or not they would like to retake the exam in an attempt to get a higher grade.

THE (IM)POSSIBILITIES OF SCHOOL SUCCESS

I begin my examination of the (im)possibilities of the reframing activities utilized in Megan's School Success class with a focus on student agency. As I deconstruct the

89

significance of these self-help activities, I find that these activities both encourage and discourage student agency. The self-help activities affirm students' agency in that they teach the students that they have the ability to determine their school and life outcomes. Moreover, the school success curriculum and Megan's pedagogical practices are transformative in nature. At the heart of the school success activities is the idea that students can transform what is seemingly a negative scenario into a positive one. No doubt, these student-centered activities are in stark contrast to the experiences they had in their previous high schools where they did not see themselves or their experiences reflected in the curriculum at all, and they were provided little to no opportunities to exercise their agency in an effort to confront and transform the issues that contributed to their school achievement outcomes. At Esplanade, and especially in the school success classes, students see their lived experiences and social identities as integral components of the curriculum. Moreover, the self-help activities encourage students to open up, share, confront, and overcome the problems they have in their lives so they can be successful academically as well as in life outside of school. Because Esplanade students generally do well academically, graduate from high school, enter the job market, and/or go on to college, the transformative approach at Esplanade and Megan's School Success class, provides a counter narrative to the student pathology ideology that makes Esplanade out to be no more than a holding cell that prolongs students' eventual incarceration.

However, in so much as there are possibilities with the school success curriculum, the self-help activities may also undermine students' agency. As I continue to unpack the significance of these activities, we can see that the student agency that is promoted in the school success curriculum, in the end, may be a form of constrained student agency in that students are positioned as passive when they confront their problems. Essentially, the students' choices are to 1) accept things the way they are in their lives and be unsuccessful (e.g., live in misery, not do good in school) or 2) recast their problems in a more positive light, and as a result, be successful in school and life. It is important to realize that the work students do to recast their problems into a more positive light is simply mind work. It is as if students put on rose-colored glasses to see things more brightly but they do not do anything to actually confront/transform the problems they face. As such, this approach to student agency does not provide any strategies for resisting, fighting back, transforming oppressive structures, organizing with others to protest, or leaving the situation, but rather, pushes students to accept things the way they are. This is especially evident in the handout, "I'm Only Really Happy When I'm Miserable," which specifically states, "There is power in accepting things as they are, in not judging it to be good or bad until we see how things turn out. Many times we make ourselves miserable by looking at things as 'awful'." From this lesson, students learn that they are not only responsible for their own misery, but they are encouraged to just accept things the way they are, and simply change their outlook.

Also worth examining is the idea that students can liberate themselves from the problems they encounter. Since many of the problems that students face are deeply rooted in social systems of oppression, it is unlikely that this oppression will ever disappear; thus it is misleading to suggest that the students can disband themselves from these oppressions. Thompson's (1997) examination of the problem-centered approach is helpful here. In her work, Thompson differentiates the problem-centered approach from the concept of trouble. According to Thompson, trouble, unlike problems, is an ongoing part of everyday life that communities of color face (e.g., racism). For people of color, trouble is not a deviation from the norm, but rather is the norm. From the perspective of trouble, the problem-centered approach is not helpful because students are misled to believe that they can solve their problems and live problem-free lives. Whereas the trouble perspective sees trouble as out there and inevitable, the problem-centered approach sees problems as internal and fixable. As such, the problem-centered approach leads students to approaches that focus on themselves to solve the perceived problems instead of focusing on the systems of oppression that cause those problems. Because the School Success class utilizes a problem-centered approach, it has students focusing internally to fix their problems instead of developing strategies to deal with the external troubles they must inevitably deal with and learn how to be successful despite ongoing trouble.

Further, because Megan's students focus internally to address their problems, they are not provided any strategies to individually or collectively confront systems of marginalization. In fact, Megan takes pride in the fact that her students do not build forces along or across ethnic/racial lines. This becomes clear, for example, when Megan talks with her students about her recent visit to a traditional high school in town that also schools large numbers of students of color. Megan states:

> Megan: When I went to Mustang High School, it was apparent to me that the students walked down the halls in their own ethnic groups. Like all the African Americans and all the Caucasians and all the Hispanics would be walking together. And take a look around you here. None of you are sitting with someone from your same ethnic group. You're all sitting with someone else. And you chose to do that. I didn't give you a seating chart. There are some students that still hang out in their groups here at this school, but hats off to you. Good job! You ought to be proud of yourselves.

Megan's admiration of student integration here takes up the colorblind perspective (Nieto & Bode, 2012). The colorblind perspective has it that students are just students and that race should be insignificant, irrelevant, and even imperceptible in educational experiences. The colorblind perspective fails to recognize the ways in which students, despite any attempts to integrate in their school setting, do experience racial oppression. By priding herself and her students' apparent integration, Megan credits her students' integration efforts to overcome "their" race problems that students of color face otherwise and elsewhere (such as at the high school Megan visited). In extension, this argument has it that students who do not integrate (e.g., those at the traditional high school) are responsible for their own strife within the educational system—again an approach that internalizes student achievement problems instead of confronting the external forces that impact student achievement. With the emphasis on "self," students are discouraged from understanding their problems as embedded in structures, institutions and social ideologies that affect not only themselves, but others within and across racial groups.

Cammarota (2016) gets at this point in his own case study of high school students who confront social justice issues at an Arizona high school in the Tucson Unified School District (TUSD). In his work, Cammarota encourages students to take on the work of addressing and transforming the issues that impact their educational achievement—as is the case in Megan's School Success class. However, he warns that students must be careful not to confuse the symptoms of these problems with the actual root causes of the problems. In his case study, Cammarota explains, "students learn that focusing on symptoms will only lead to a superficial and ineffective understanding of the problem because the root causes will remain unchallenged and unchanged" (p. 93). As an example, Cammarota looks to the theme of racially or ethnically based curricular tracking in schools. He emphasizes that what are often identified as problems in students' academic achievement (e.g., absenteeism, disengagement, failure, dropping out, and segregation)—issues that position the student as the source of the problem—are actually symptoms to the problem, not the problems themselves. Once we stop looking at symptoms as problems and start to identify the root causes of school achievement, Cammarota argues, we will begin to identify how issues of "power, colonization, and racism represent[ed] the foundation or "roots" of problems" (p. 93). As Cammarota explains, once students recognize the roots to problems, they can stop looking at themselves as the source and solution to the problem they encounter and start to look for solutions that are entrenched in their social environments. Needless to say, when students start to look at the root causes of their educational achievement, their methods for confronting and transforming these problems necessarily change. Whereas a symptom approach has students trying to fix themselves (as is the case with the self-help activities in Megan's school success class), an approach that focuses on the root causes of the problems has students confronting and transforming their social environments where these problems emerge.

As an example of students engaged in this type of work, Cammarrota (2016) details a case study of high school students enrolled in the Social Justice Education Project (SJEP) at a high school in TUSD. These high school students participated in Youth Participatory Action Research (YPAR) projects which required each student to conduct a qualitative research study that focused on social justice issues they and their peers faced that limited their potential. By utilizing qualitative research methods such as participant observations, interviewing, and photo and video documentation, these students generated key patterns and themes that they first wrote about in poems. Instead of working individually, the students then worked collectively to identify generative themes that emerged across students' poems. As a result of this collective experience, students were able to identify themes such as racism, discrimination, immigration, and political movements that were represented across students' poems and research. In the end, the students created a skit that pulled directly from the racist incidents they recorded in their field notes, one of which was called the "Spanish Disadvantage". In this skit, students dramatized in front of a live audience how the students were frequently reprimanded for speaking Spanish in school. As Cammarota explains, "Because the skit connects people directly to the meaning and experience of the "Spanish Disadvantage," it gives them a sense, in a dramatic way, of how disadvantaged students may feel" (p. 100). At the end of the year, students present their research studies and their skit to parents and community members. It is through these presentations and through the relationships that are formed across students, parents, and community members that they collectively confront and transform oppressive practices such as being reprimanded for speaking Spanish.

If we go back to the self-help activities that Megan implements in her school success class, such as the negative scenario presented in the final exam that describes a student's mom who has a drinking problem and is chronically absent from the house, we can see that what is being identified as the problems in this scenario (e.g., mom obsessively drinks, does not care, does not meet her responsibilities) may actually be the symptoms/outcomes to larger social justice issues that this mom faces in the workplace, in her previous schooling experiences, and in her larger social context (e.g., being underpaid, overworked, discriminated against based on race, class, gender, immigration status, and language use; coupled with limited opportunities to seek employment elsewhere due to her low educational obtainment that resulted from school inequities that are likely very similar to those her child is currently facing). When the focus is directed on these larger issues of power and discrimination in education and the work force, the way an individual confronts the problem also changes. In this case, instead of the student focusing internally on how s/he can change her/his perspective on the mom's seeming negative behavior, or internalizing the problems as the mom's inability to deal with stress effectively, students, and perhaps parents, can address the external social justice issues they face in their schooling and working contexts.

From this analysis, we can see that there are both possibilities and impossibilities in the school success curriculum and in Megan's pedagogical practices. On a positive note, the ideology of self-help does not stigmatize students with traditional deficiency labels (e.g., remedial, at-risk, pathological) that they commonly encounter in traditional high schools. Rather, students are depicted as being successful and are encouraged to employ their own agency in order to actualize their success, including defining what success means for them academically. This is especially apparent in the policies that allow students to determine when they are ready to take tests and when they are satisfied with their grades. However, at the same time the self-help activities that are meant to empower students by providing them strategies to develop positive perspectives, also encourage the students to be passive individuals—to accept things the way they are. This can be a dangerous way to approach a system that intends to squash their dreams of success and has no vision of their lives outside of incarceration.

In this chapter I have elaborated on and brought light to the complexity of Megan's multicultural practices, and as such, we can see that Megan does not embody a monolithic notion of multicultural education; her work is not unilaterally progressing toward a fully-formed idea of what multicultural education is. Because Megan's pedagogical practices are shaped by various conflicting ideologies, her multicultural work takes up and reflects these ideologies. Thus, even when Megan and the larger school context at Esplanade are well-intentioned and geared toward success, the ideology of White superiority, student pathology, and school success shape the (im)possibilities of multicultural education in a complex way. Despite Megan's best intentions to advocate for her students, her pedagogical practices work towards contradictory ends. These findings are critical to the field of multicultural education wherein the concept of the idealized, rugged multicultural education teacher often serves as a prototype for all teachers to work toward.

CONCLUSION

This study has involved an investigation into the pedagogical practices of three White teachers who are committed to the project of implementing multicultural education in their classrooms and schools. As a researcher I sought to understand what was pedagogically possible for teachers who are embedded in sociopolitical contexts that, among other things, are anti-immigrant, anti-bilingual, and pro-White American. In this final chapter I discuss the findings I presented in the individual case study chapters in an attempt to advance suggestions for what educators can gain from these data as a whole. I conduct this discussion through a series of questions I pose below. These questions include: What can we learn from case studies?; What brought the teachers to multicultural education?; How did the teachers approach multicultural education; What (im)possibilities emerged from the teachers' multicultural practices?; What are the best multicultural practices?; What is the significance of this study?; and, Is it all worth it?

WHAT CAN WE LEARN FROM CASE STUDIES?

There were various ways I could have organized and presented the data in this book. For example, I could have identified major themes that emerged and ran across the three teachers' pedagogical practices and organized chapters according to these themes. This type of organization would have involved discussing all of the teachers in each chapter and explain how particular themes played out in each of their teaching contexts. Instead of this approach, or any other option, I chose to present individual case studies of participating teachers because each school and teacher was embedded in a sociopolitical context that varied from the others and each teacher had a unique approach to confronting social justice issues. When taken together, the (im)possibilities for multicultural education for each teacher emerged differently and could be best represented in individual case studies. In developing the case studies, I was able to contextualize the teachers' pedagogical practices in their local ideological fields and unpack the significance of the ways they negotiated, contested, and reified the sociopolitical contexts they were embedded in. By contextualizing the teachers' practices, we gain a better understanding of why particular pedagogical practices emerged over possible others. Thus, the aim of presenting the data in individual case studies was not to suggest that there were no connections or similarities among the data presented in each chapter, but rather to highlight the distinctiveness of the teachers' sociopolitical contexts and multicultural practices.

WHAT BROUGHT THE TEACHERS TO MULTICULTURAL EDUCATION?

The teachers' motivations for confronting and transforming social justice issues through their multicultural pedagogies emerged differently for each teacher. Uniquely, Megan did not come to Esplanade with a multicultural agenda. Before coming to Esplanade, Megan was largely unaware of how concepts of race and social class ideologically and structurally shape inequitable life chances for people. It was not until Megan began working at Esplanade that she started to question the assumptions and normalcy of the white superiority ideology. Thus, for Megan, it was through her teaching experiences at Esplanade that led her to contest these views and served as the impetus for Megan's multicultural practices.

In contrast to Megan, Ms. DeGraw and Mr. Potts entered their schooling contexts with a multicultural agenda already in mind. Both Ms. DeGraw and Mr. Potts had life experiences outside of and prior to becoming teachers that informed their agendas to confront and transform the inequities their students were facing. For Ms. DeGraw, she had many life experiences in which she was either silenced or made to feel invisible as a woman, lesbian, and religious minority. These experiences fueled her ambition to confront and transform a schooling system that marginalizes ESL students in much the same way she had been and continues to be marginalized.

Mr. Potts similarly had life experiences that serve as the backdrop for his critical perspective and advocacy for his Latinx students. Because Mr. Potts was schooled in South America where he occupied the roles of ethnic and language minority, he was able to draw from these experiences to craft his own transformative multicultural practices in his classroom. Also, because Mr. Potts worked as a bilingual teacher in other schools for many years prior to coming to Viewpoint Elementary, he came to his teaching position at Viewpoint Elementary with presuppositions about which bilingual program most effectively addresses the inequitable educational experiences Latinx students often endure. From this prior knowledge, Mr. Pott's brought the two-way dual language model into his classroom. Although a clearly modified version of the dual language programs he worked in before, he nonetheless tried his best to apply the logic of the dual language program in his stand-alone classroom.

Regardless of the varied life and teaching experiences that the teachers in this study had, their multicultural teaching agendas were very similar: to provide equitable educational experiences to students of color in a site of public education. Also, to varying degrees and in various ways, the students at all school sites included in this study were ideologically produced as deficient and/or pathological in the larger social setting. In order to address these equity issues, the participating teachers approached multicultural education in different ways.

HOW DID THE TEACHERS APPROACH MULTICULTURAL EDUCATION?

For the most part, Megan positioned herself as a learner in that she provided opportunities for her students to teach her about social justice issues. As I explained in chapter 4, this learner approach challenged traditional teacher-student power relations. The disruption of traditional teaching and learning roles in Megan's School Success class was consistent with the alternative practices of the larger school that attempted to break down traditional teacher-student power relations. Through various school policies and practices, Esplanade students and teachers shared resources, school facilities, and responsibilities for teaching and learning.

Unlike Megan, Ms. DeGraw's approach to implementing multicultural education was much more confrontational and with a sense of certainty about what is educationally right or wrong for her ESL students. For example, instead of seeking to gain racial knowledge from her students' perspectives as Megan did, Ms. DeGraw started with the premise that her students were being discriminated against and wanted to bring attention to this in a public way. We saw evidence of this in Ms. DeGraw's attempts to shine a light on ESL students' experiences at Drew Middle School in the production of the school orientation video and the posting of students' work at the entrance of the school. She also directly confronted teachers about racial incidents her students reported to her and confronted teachers and administrators at staff meetings, such as when she publicly criticized the practice of exclusively including White students and Christian cultural practices in the school assemblies.

Mr. Pott's approach to integrating multicultural practices was yet again different from that of Megan's and Ms. DeGraw's. Whereas Megan can be thought of as primarily a learner in her multicultural endeavors and Ms. DeGraw as an aggressive challenger to the status quo, Mr. Potts can be thought of as someone who tries to make change through functional relationships. In Mr. Pott's attempts to advocate for his Latinx Spanish-speaking students, he did not address the faculty members at his school aggressively about the matter, as was more of Ms. DeGraw's approach. Rather, he found that he could make progress in better serving his Latinx, Spanish-speaking students by establishing functional relationships in his school community. This was evident when Viewpoint Elementary was considering to adopt a school-wide dual language program. No doubt, there was nothing more that Mr. Potts wanted than to have a school-wide dual-language program at Viewpoint Elementary. However, in the end, Mr. Potts voted against the implementation of the program. Knowing that most other teachers did not support the program and were going to vote against the program, Mr. Pott's vote against the program was his way of expressing the realization that a school-wide dual-language program was not going to work in a school where teachers did not work together in support of the program. He believed that teachers needed to form relationships and collaboratively fight for students' rights in order to achieve equitable educational outcomes. When these relationships failed to form at Viewpoint Elementary, Mr. Potts quit his job and sought a position at a local elementary school that did accept the district grant to implement a school-wide dual language program and where relationships could be formed to collectively advocate for Latinx students.

Mr. Pott's decision to leave Viewpoint Elementary and not force a bilingual program on teachers who did not want it was also a means of cultivating relationships between Viewpoint Elementary teachers and students. Mr. Potts thought it was better to promote relationships between the anti-bilingual White teachers and their Latinx, Spanish-speaking students than to stay at Viewpoint Elementary and fight for a program that would likely fail and foster further teacher resentment toward the Latinx, Spanish-speaking students. Not only did he think that the Latinx, Spanish-speaking students would be better served at Viewpoint Elementary without a dual-language program, but he also thought that his multicultural and bilingual education ambitions would be more effective if he were to work in a school where he would be part of a network of pro-bilingual education teachers. Thus, for Mr. Potts, the possibility for multicultural education lies in teachers' abilities to build relationships with each other and with their students.

Mr. Pott's "get along" approach to multicultural education also frames how he confronted a school system that excluded his Latinx students from fully participating in school activities. Mr. Pott's multicultural practices often worked by getting along and finding opportunities within an already defined school system. Sometimes this meant finding possibilities within the ambiguities of the school system. This was the case, for example, when Mr. Potts submitted poem entries for his Spanish-dominant students to poetry contests. Mr. Potts was aware that the poetry contests were intended for English language submissions only, even though the official rules never stipulated so. Instead of directly confronting the poem committees or the larger school about changing this exclusionary practice, he strategically took advantage of the vague rules by submitting poems in Spanish and proceeded from there in trying to get the Spanish submissions accepted. Mr. Pott's approach to multicultural education worked from the standpoint that he will not be able to change the system, especially when surrounded by educators who are not on board for such change, so he had to find ways of working within the already defined system. Mr. Pott's knowledge and approach to implementing multicultural education was likely the result of many years of experience in serving Latinx, Spanish-speaking students in bilingual programs, and realizing what multicultural (im)possibilities lie in the current educational system.

WHAT (IM)POSSIBILITIES EMERGED FROM THE TEACHERS' MULTICULTURAL PRACTICES?

The teachers approached multicultural education in different ways and in each case the teachers experienced varied instances of success and failure at doing so. Through the lens of the (im)possible multicultural teacher, the case studies demonstrated how the teachers' multicultural practices showed much promise, but were also constrained by the sociopolitical context in which they were teaching.

Even at Esplanade, which is considered a progressive school that utilized many alternative practices in order to promote school success, the self-help curriculum nonetheless downplayed the power the sociopolitical context had in producing the problems students faced in their academics, at the same time it undermined the students' agency to confront such problems. As a result, the self-help activities did not provide students the tools or strategies they needed to negotiate this sociopolitical context and make changes at the root level of the problems they were confronting. In contrasting ways, the self-help activities utilized in the school success class simultaneously constructed students as academically capable and in charge of their academic achievement outcomes and conversely positioned students as the culprits of their problems and as passive in transforming the larger social, structural, and ideological issues that gave rise to these problems. Moreover, Megan's approach to confronting her own racism worked towards contradictory ends. While Megan positioned her students as knowledgeable as she sought their advice on issues of race and racism, she concurrently reestablished the racial status quo and oppressive power relations between teacher/student and White/other when she identified herself as a racist and asked her students to provide evidence of such.

At Drew Middle School, deficiency ideologies constructed ESL students as remedial and invisible due to their perceived deficiencies in language and culture. The deficiency ideology and rendering of ESL students as invisible worked in tandem at this school to communicate the message that ESL students did not gain "official" student status or visibility until they overcame their perceived cultural and linguistic deficits. Through Ms. DeGraw's attempts to bring visibility to her ESL students' cultural and linguistic attributes, she successfully interrupted the dominant ideologies circulating in the school that rendered these student qualities invisible. At the same time however, in bringing visibility to these qualities, she may have been reinforcing her students' invisibility by suggesting to the larger school that her students had not overcome those perceived deficits. This may have been the case in the class mural and story activity when Ms. DeGraw displayed ESL students' cultural stories and drawings to the larger school.

There were also instances when Ms. DeGraw's attempts to interrupt the status quo by bringing visibility to her students' cultural and linguistic qualities may have resulted in sustaining the status quo. For example, when Ms. DeGraw tried to bring visibility to ESL students' experiences of marginalization at Drew Middle School through the production of a school orientation video that solicited ESL students' voices on this matter, the ESL students either stayed quiet or denied that they had experienced incidents of marginalization. Additionally, when Ms. DeGraw solicited written student feedback on her ESL classes, students never recognized or expressed appreciation for Ms. DeGraw's attempts to implement Spanish instruction or any of the other multicultural practices. Instead, the students emphasized several times over that they preferred more English instruction and ideally would like to be transferred out of ESL classes altogether. These student responses may be a reflection that Ms. DeGraw's ESL students internalized the deficit ideologies that told them that they needed to overcome perceived cultural and linguistic deficits in order to gain visibility and participate in the normalized academic activities reserved for the White, English-speaking students at Drew Middle School. Thus, students' responses to Ms. DeGraw's attempts to affirm their cultural and linguistic identities as well as her attempts to bring visibility to their experiences of marginalization, are reasonable given that the school and larger society defined these students in deficit terms. The students seemed to realize that English was the key to progress not only at Drew Middle School, but in the United States. As such, students elected for more English instruction over the activities in which Ms. DeGraw attempted to affirm and bring visibility to their cultural and linguistic qualities.

At Viewpoint Elementary, Latinx, Spanish-dominant students were also produced as deficient and were marginalized due to their lack of fluency in the English language. Even though Mr. Potts tried to counter this by implementing a makeshift dual language program in his classroom, he nonetheless reinforced the notion that White, English-speaking students' educational needs were to take priority. This manifested in a variety of ways: speaking more English than Spanish, delivering content in English first, using sheltered English, and utilizing translation sheets to appease English-speaking parents. Moreover, the student selection process that determined who would be enrolled in Mr. Potts' class worked against the goals of any dual language model. Instead of providing an even playing field where no student would be considered "remedial" simply due to the label of being a "language learner," the selection process reinstated a remedial status to Latinx, Spanish-speaking students due to the students' unparalleled academic proficiencies, especially students' reading levels.

If we take the teachers' pedagogical practices at face value, we may easily perceive them as failures at multicultural education. Take Mr. Potts, for example, who voted against a bilingual education program that was being proposed by the alternative languages office at the school district. Framed in the traditional agent-centered approach to multicultural education, I can imagine that the district administrators, or any other educators for that matter, did not think of Mr. Potts as a multicultural teacher. However, this study focuses on what is pedagogically possible, given the sociopolitical context in which teachers work. By examining Mr. Pott's practices from the framework of the (im)possible multicultural teacher, we can see that Mr. Pott's pedagogical practices cannot be easily classified as successful or not successful because they are imbued with contradictions. In short, his pedagogical practices both supported and interrupted the inequities he confronted. By voting against the implementation of the dual language program, he and other teachers further cemented a subtractive schooling system that promoted school success at the expense of students' language and culture. At the same time, however, Mr. Potts left this subtractive schooling context to go teach at an additive school where he could promote the Spanish language in addition to the English language.

WHAT ARE THE BEST MULTICULTURAL PRACTICES?

Even though ideologies of deficiency operated in various ways at all three schools involved in this study, it would be misleading to assume that there is a set of "best" practices that could successfully omit these deficit ideologies from any of the schooling contexts. All of the teachers in this study worked toward implementing transformative multicultural practices—practices that aimed to transform deficit ideologies and inequitable structural factors in schools. However, the teachers' efforts resulted in what could only be considered a partial transformation. With this being said, I cannot say that there is a set of "best" practices that the teachers implemented or should have ideally implemented. The idea of "best" practices assumes that there is a one-size-fits-all approach to multicultural education, which ultimately leads to essentializing "right" ways teachers can achieve educational equity. Each case study chapter detailed a teacher's distinct practices, what might be considered best practices for a particular teacher's circumstances, but they should not be considered universal "best" practices that could be applied across teaching contexts. The findings presented in the case studies of this book speak to the range and depth to which multicultural education can be implemented, but the (im)possibilities for multicultural practices are as diverse as are the teachers, students, and sociopolitical contexts they are embedded in. Thus, any given multicultural practice has potential (im)possibilities. Through the (im)possible multicultural lens, it is assumed that a teacher cannot implement ideal multicultural practices or permanently change the racial status quo.

WHAT IS THE SIGNIFICANCE OF THIS STUDY?

First, let me reiterate that my take on multicultural education research is that it overly reifies the idea that multicultural teachers are self-made. As I discussed in chapter one, the concept of the rugged multicultural teacher assumes that teachers just have to work hard and be committed to a multicultural agenda in order to actualize their multicultural practices and gain their status as a multicultural teacher. As can be imagined, this popular agent-centered approach to multicultural education—what I have conceptualized as the rugged multicultural teacher—can be problematic for teachers who may come to believe that they are the sole factor in determining the success or failure in implementing multicultural education in their K-12 classrooms. Equipped with the "rugged multicultural teacher mentality," teachers may enter the teaching field with grand ideas of transformation and being able to single-handedly achieve the promise of educational equity for all students. Disillusioned about what can actually be achieved and underestimating their own complicity in the inequitable power relations that operate within schools and society, teachers are ill-prepared to deal with the eminent struggles, contradictions, and failures they will encounter as they attempt to implement multicultural education. Consequently, when teachers struggle to implement multicultural pedagogies and curriculum, they may only look to themselves as the source of the problems in implementing multicultural education. Needless to say, teachers can become overburdened with feelings of frustration, powerlessness, and self-blame. I do not think that it is much of a stretch to think that teachers' low self-assessment in terms of value and effectiveness contributes to the high turnover rate that occurs in teachers' first few years of being in the teaching profession.

In this book I critique the agent-centered approach to multicultural education, because it simply does not map onto teachers' actual multicultural teaching practices. It does not take into consideration what is pedagogically (im)possible in an inequitable social context. Without contextualizing teachers' multicultural work, we end up essentializing what an ideal form of multicultural education should look like. With that being said, the data presented in this book is qualitatively significant because it provides several portraits of what teachers can reasonably do in their attempts to confront and transform racial inequalities in their schools.

The case studies in this book also offer implications that are far reaching for teacher education programs. First, teacher education programs need to foster a critical lens of schooling that provides strategies for students to identify the sociopolitical contexts that define particular school practices and policies. Class readings that take up Critical Multicultural Education, Critical Race Theory, Critical Media Literacy, Critical Literacy, Whiteness Studies, and Social Justice Education offer much in cultivating this critical perspective. In addition to critical course readings, the findings from the data in this book call for more fieldwork. Students need to see the daily grind of teaching so they can realize the (im)possibilities for multicultural education. I speculate that preservice teachers would benefit from field work experiences that ask them to identify and analyze the sociopolitical context of their assigned school. To this end, preservice teachers should be asked to keep journals of their observations so they can gain the experiences themselves of identifying various elements that make up the sociopolitical context and then from there theorize the multicultural (im)possibilities.

Another helpful strategy that can be utilized in teacher education programs is the fostering of teacher collaborations. By encouraging teachers to do their multicultural work in relationship with others, teachers may disconnect from the concept of rugged individualism that has teachers assume that multicultural practices are simply a product of individual effort. By working together, teachers can collaboratively strategize multicultural practices for particular school contexts. With this being said, it may be an effective strategy to place preservice teachers in pairs or small groups with a mentor teacher. Working in relationships with other teachers also holds promise for the possibility that teachers can support each other's multicultural agendas and provide feedback to each other on how they may make progress in developing multicultural practices in particular school sites. As I showed in Mr. Pott's case study, he felt most successful when he worked in relationships with other pro-bilingual teachers.

IS IT ALL WORTH IT?

In presenting the data included in this book, I have hammered the point that despite teachers' efforts and ambitions of multicultural education, no ideal can be reasonably achieved. Even in the best-case scenario, teachers may end up reinforcing the school inequities they seek to transform and feeling unsuccessful. As a reminder, Mr. Potts did not consider himself to be a "successful" teacher. Given these findings, it may be reasonable to ask, "What is the use?; "How can teachers know if they are making a difference?"; How do teachers know if they are being a successful multicultural teacher?; Is it all worth it?

After reading this book, readers may believe that the project of multicultural education is futile or that it may be too difficult to determine with any certainty whether educators are making progress towards quality multicultural practices. As discussed in the case study chapters, even the teachers' most promising multicultural education practices are not convincingly "successful". As such, no clear "success" stories emerge from the data and it does not seem to be the case that the teachers are making progress towards certain steps, stages, or defined multicultural goals. Rather, what emerges from the case studies are teachers' ongoing struggles to advocate for their students. This may be disheartening when we consider that the teachers featured in this book are hard working individuals who are committed to the project of multicultural education as a means to address social justice issues. One may ask, if these teachers were not successful, "what hope do we have for teachers who are not fully committed to the project of multicultural education"?

As I have argued throughout this book, the field of education is too entrenched in binary concepts of success and failure that define teachers as either good teachers or bad teachers or racist teachers or non-racist teachers. It is my position that hard-working, committed multicultural teachers occupy both sides of this binary. They are simply both. Thus, instead of seeking to understand or determine whether teachers are successful or not in their multicultural practices, we should encourage teachers and researchers to embrace the complexity, and at times ambiguity, of the multicultural work teachers do. To this end, we are in need of a new vocabulary that captures teachers' complex multicultural practices. I offer the term "the (im)possible multicultural teacher," but surely there are many more terms that could capture the complex multicultural work teachers do.

It is my recommendation that in reading and making conclusions about the data included in this book, that one does so with a critical lens concerning what can be achieved in terms of multicultural education. It has been my argument all along that the teachers would not achieve any ideal form of multicultural education, but rather that they would be involved in constant struggles to better serve their students of color. This understanding of the teachers' multicultural work does not mean that the teachers did not effectively advocate for their students or that their efforts were a waste of time. Even though the teachers who are featured in this book did not reach any idealized form of multicultural education, I nonetheless believe that their efforts were worthy and contributed to improving the quality of education their students received. Their work was indeed worth it!

APPENDIX

METHODOLOGY

The central goal in this book is to understand how the sociopolitical context of schooling shapes the (im)possibilities of multicultural education of three white teachers. With this goal in mind, I utilized a research methodology that would allow me to gain access to the teachers' everyday working contexts where their pedagogical practices took shape and were delivered. Furthermore, because I wanted to come to some kind of understanding of the sociopolitical context teachers were embedded in and how that shaped the complexity of their pedagogical practices, it was crucial that I spend large amounts of time with the teachers in their natural work settings. For these purposes, I conducted a qualitative research study and utilized ethnographic research methods. This research allowed me to work closely and for long periods of time with a small number of participants. As Crenshaw (2014) states, a qualitative, ethnographic research design allows for a holistic account, in which "researchers try to develop a complex picture of the problem or issue under study. This involves reporting multiple perspectives, identifying the many factors involved in a situation, and generally sketching the larger picture that emerges" (p. 186). Essentially, an ethnographic research study allows the researcher to gain an insider's perspective by incorporating her or himself into the research site for extended periods of time as he/ she actively participates in the daily activities of all the participants while attending to specific research questions. As a result of my extended time in the participating teachers' classrooms and schools, I was able to provide a "thick description" (Fetterman, 2010) of the teachers, their classrooms, and their teaching practices, which is detailed in the individual case study chapters. This thick description is no doubt my interpretation of the data, which emerged as the result of my collaboration with the participating teachers. The process of interpretation, however, remains open-ended as readers are not only invited to critique my analysis, they are also welcome to formulate their own.

SELECTION OF PARTICIPANTS

The process of selecting teachers to participate in this study began by identifying "successful multicultural teachers" or teachers who were committed to multicultural education and/or addressing social justice issues in their classrooms. This process involved my own networking with teachers, school administrators, and teacher educators. Thus, instead of choosing teachers randomly, I sought the advice of other educators to identify who stood out as exemplary multicultural teachers. As a result of this selection process, the participating teachers in this study emerged

105

as "model" multicultural teachers among their peers and mentors. It is important to point out that the goals of this research project were modified after the selection of the participants was completed and data collection had begun. Initially, this research project started off with the goal of examining "successful" multicultural teachers. My hope was to share the teaching experiences of "successful" multicultural teachers with other educators so they may be able to garner ideas for implementing effective multicultural teaching practices. No doubt, I embraced the "multicultural"-"not multicultural" dichotomy when I first started this research project. While educators can certainly still learn from the participating teachers' multicultural practices, my notions of "success" and "multicultural" were contested as I engaged in the fieldwork and learned from the teachers. Thus, even though my network of educators helped me identify "successful" multicultural teachers, I quickly learned that the teachers themselves did not identify as such. Rather, the teachers often described themselves as "struggling" and "frustrated". During my first meeting with Mr. Potts, for example, he was forthright in telling me that he was not a "good teacher". Indeed, there were many occasions when the teachers' practices did not reflect the "success" they had hoped for in their attempts of reaching their own multicultural goals. In fact, in some cases teachers were seemingly working against their multicultural goals.

Importantly, as my data collection evolved, so did my research inquiries. Crenshaw (2014) points out that this is one of the benefits of using a qualitative research design: Qualitative research allows for an emergent design which means that the research design, including the research questions, emerge and evolve as data is being collected. This research process is referred to as grounded theory—a process in which theories emerge from the ongoing interaction between data collection and data analysis (Charmaz, 2014). With that being said, I did not start off with predetermined hypotheses about how teachers would implement multicultural practices, but rather with broad research inquiries about "successful" multicultural teachers that evolved as I collected and analyzed data. As I weaved data analysis with data collection, I found that early data analysis informed the direction of future data collection and theorizing of that data. In her description of grounded theory, Charmaz (2014) succinctly explains, "…researchers construct a theory 'grounded' in their data" (p. 1).

The process of securing teachers to participate in this study was multifaceted. Once a teacher was identified through organic conversations I had with educators at all levels of public education, I then took the steps necessary to meet the teachers and introduce myself and the research study. I first set up a time to meet with each prospective teacher in their classrooms after school. After I introduced myself and provided an overview of my research study, I simply asked the teachers if I could be a guest in their classrooms during the day, with no commitment to participate in my study. Before I even formally asked if the teachers would participate in my study, I took the time to get to know them, their students, and their classroom settings. I actually did not sit down and take notes until I had worked in their classrooms for 6 to 8 weeks, which allowed time for students and teachers to know who I was and become comfortable with my presence in the classroom. After this initial 6–8 week period, I was able to comfortably take notes while in the classroom without being positioned as an awkward outsider. It was at this point that I asked the teachers if they would like to participate in my study. When a teacher agreed to participate in this study, I then started to visit their classrooms as well as other school contexts more regularly. During these visits I began to take field notes and conduct interviews. Once the data collection phase was initiated, I remained in the teachers' classrooms for a little over a year and maintained relationships with each teacher after the data collection ended. Working from grounded theory, my goal was to remain in the classrooms long enough to reach "saturation," a point at which collecting additional data would not result in any new findings or themes (Charmaz, 2014). As I explained in chapter 5, I chose to write up the data in individual case studies for each teacher in an effort to show the distinctiveness of each teacher and school site. As Yin (2014) explains, case studies are effective in that they "allow investigators to focus on a "case" and retain a holistic and real-world perspective" (p. 4). In all, the ethnographic tools I used to collect data included participant-observations, formal interviews, and informal interviews. In what follows, I discuss each of these ethnographic research methods in detail.

PARTICIPANT OBSERVATION

One of the primary ways I was able to identify some of the ideologies and instances of teacher advocacy was by spending large amounts of time interacting in each teaching context. I found participant observations proved to be the most effective way of embedding myself in the research context and interacting with teachers. A participant-observer is a researcher who participates in the social setting of the research site yet maintains his or her capacity as a researcher (Spradley, 1980; Emerson, Fretz, & Shaw, 2011). As a participant-observer in the teachers' classrooms (among other settings that included faculty meetings, faculty lunchroom, student cafeteria, afterschool activities, and recess), I was able to move in and out of spaces where I occupied the role of both participant and observer.

In order to gain an understanding of the nuances that make up each teachers' classroom, my participant-observation sessions involved interchangeably taking notes on the research setting and fully participating with all the members at each school site. A careful balance between taking ethnographic notes and interacting with the members of the research setting was critical to achieve, as I was simultaneously trying to build relationships and collect research data. With these goals in mind, I put close to equal amounts of time into observing and participating in each classroom.

As a way to participate in the everyday class activities with the teachers and their students, I volunteered as a teacher's aide twice a week in 2-hour sessions for each of my participants' classrooms. During this time, I read to students, graded student papers, copied assignments, facilitated small groups of students in completing class activities and assignments, worked as a translator in the Spanish and English languages, worked one-on-one with students on assignments and class activities, and facilitated in carrying out everyday activities, such as taking students to recess or lunch or staying after school with them. During this time in which I worked as a teacher's aide, I established relationships with students and teachers. Everyone knew me by name and came to depend on my presence in the classroom.

This part of my data collection was critical in that my role as a participant in the classroom allowed me to develop reciprocal relationships with the teachers, allowed a smooth entry into the research sites, and enriched my knowledge of the day-to-day happenings in each classroom. By working in the classroom, I demonstrated to teachers that I was invested in their multicultural projects and I was not there only to take from them. It was important to me that our relationships be reciprocal: I gave to them by working in their classes and by giving them feedback on concepts they were working on, and they helped me by informing me of the processes they were involved in as they attempted to implement multicultural education.

In addition to the sessions when I participated in the classroom as a teacher's aide, I also visited each classroom twice a week for 2 hours each visit for a little over a period of a year in the capacity of a "researcher". During these sessions, I arrived to the classrooms with a notebook and pen, familiarized myself with the day's activities, and positioned myself in close proximity to where the students and teacher were interacting, often sitting at the same table or among the same desks as the students. Because I wanted to understand the nuances that make multicultural education both possible and impossible to achieve, I tried to pay attention to aspects of the research site that would help me understand the complexity of the teachers' pedagogical practices. Not knowing what would be relevant, I tried to keep my senses open to the many activities that were occurring in each teacher's classroom. During my visits, I paid close attention to and took notes on dialogue, movement, curriculum, teacher-student interactions, teacher-teacher-interactions, teacher-researcher interactions, nonverbal communication, and the physical environment of the classrooms. This process required my constant attention to what my research inquiries were and what was potentially relevant about the research site to my project. It was impossible, for example, to record everything about the research sites. Spradley (1980) refers to the process in which researchers try to remember and catalog all the information they can perceive as "overload" (p. 55). So while it may not be necessary to record how much trash is in the trash can, because there does not seem to be any relevance to my research inquiries, there are many other details in the research scene which may appear trivial at the time of the observation but then gain significance in later sessions of data analysis. For example, in my observations of Megan, details such as her not wearing makeup, jewelry, and expensive clothing, on the onset, did not seem relevant to my research inquiries. However, in later analyses, these details became key to understanding her struggle with privilege as a White, wealthy woman. Thus, my goal in writing ethnographic field notes was to include as many potentially relevant details as possible.

Even though I have discussed my participant and observation sessions as if they were two completely different activities, in reality, they were not. I only have discussed them in this way so that I can distinguish the qualities each of these related activities has to offer. In practice, they are often interconnected and cannot be considered separate activities. For example, during sessions when I was scheduled to work as an aide in the classroom (participant), I would also be observing. Most of the time I would take notes after these sessions on relevant incidents that occurred during my visits. In some cases, the class activities during my work time were so closely related to my research questions that I would stop working, grab some paper and a pen, and begin taking notes. During the sessions in which I was scheduled to observe, I was never completely a passive observer. Students and teachers would often draw me into the class discussions and activities by asking me questions, for translations, or to facilitate an activity. Many times, this class involvement meant that I needed to put my notebook and pen away so that I could become actively involved in the class activities.

FORMAL INTERVIEWS

In a continued effort to learn from the participating teachers and understand the sociopolitical contexts that made multicultural education both possible and impossible in each of the school contexts involved in this study, I conducted three (1–2 hour) formal interviews with each teacher. Formal interviews are scheduled interviews that often take place in isolated areas, and in my case, were audio-recorded. Further, formal interviews have particular goals in mind and are guided by prepared interview questions. Interviews are an important component to the ethnographic research method, because they give participants a chance to describe their own experiences and reasons for acting in certain ways (Brinkmann & Kvale, 2015). The formal interviews provided me the opportunity to learn from the teachers' first-hand experiences and perspectives. Not only did these interviews allow me to understand some of the complexity of the participants' lives and teaching experiences, they also supplemented and verified data collected during participant-observations. In this sense, sometimes the interview questions emerged from data collected during participant-observations.

When I conducted the formal interviews I asked my participants prepared questions that would help me understand what their pedagogical goals were and what impacted those goals. A brief sampling of the interview questions I asked my participants included: (a) How does your school and larger society think about the students you teach? (b) How do you respond to these beliefs? (c) Tell me about yourself? (d) What kinds of activities and community events do you participate in outside of class?, and (e) In what ways do your multicultural and antiracist beliefs become present in your classroom and other school contexts? The formal interviews included questions that were specific and focused. Even though the formal interviews were structured, this is not to say that I only received information relevant to the questions I asked. Sometimes the participants elaborated on and discussed issues beyond what I asked. This extra information was often pertinent to understanding the teachers' goals, conflicts, and so on. In every formal interview I conducted, it was important that I was an active listener, so that I could ask follow-up questions to the information the teachers provided. As such, during the formal interview sessions, I not only asked the teachers the prepared interview questions, but also follow-up questions I generated during the interview itself.

In working with Megan, for example, she had mentioned several times during my participant observations that her life had changed as a result of working at Esplanade. In a formal interview I conducted with her, I wanted her insight about this, so I asked her how her life had changed as a result of working at Esplanade. In her response she discussed how even though she has unlimited access to money, she has learned to restrict unnecessary spending and use of material goods and resources. This discussion prompted me to follow up about her casual appearance, to which she responded by talking about how she tries to maintain a certain image and that she is very open to talking to her students about her social class and struggle with racism. A portion of this interview exchange occurred as follows:

Charise: Can you tell me how your life has changed as a result of working here at Esplanade?

Megan: Um, well I have found myself, you know, even though I have unlimited cash flow, I've found myself living a lot more frugally. Just because I don't feel like it's fair or something, you know. Like I take the bus and my husband and I share a car, and we can easily have our own, you know, but it just seems stupid.

Charise: I think it's also interesting, and this is by no way like a put down or anything, but it's a surprise for me to learn that you are wealthy, because when I think of wealthy people I think about them wearing really nice clothes and all the accessories, you know. And you don't do that.

Megan: Wow! I actually take that as a compliment. I try to do that really hard. I try to maintain an image that does not show my wealth and it's good to hear that I've done that. And even though I don't show my wealth in my appearance, one of the social norms that I have broken is that I'm open about saying that I come from a wealthy background. Because most people they think if they say that, they're bragging or something, you know. And I feel like by bringing it up, it's just another thing about me. Instead of, "oh no I don't have any money". And it's interesting, because when I tell people, it throws them really off guard. They don't know what to say. And sometimes it distances me from them for a while, because they say, "Oh, you're one of them". So it's really hard, you know.

In the opening of this interview exchange I asked Megan an open-ended question, which she could have answered in any number of ways. By listening to her, I was able to follow up with a response that made a connection to my previous observation, which prompted Megan to elaborate further. By guiding the discussion, I was able to learn about another important issue that was not related to the original prepared interview question: dealing with privilege, which in her case, revealed great complexity as she physically concealed, yet verbally proclaimed her economic wealth. It is unlikely that I would have got this additional data if I had not listened to her responses and followed up with further inquiries.

Due to the formalities of these interviews, I tried to make the teachers feel as comfortable as possible. For example, the teachers decided when and where we would hold the interviews. Often times they chose to be interviewed after school or on their days off. The locations they chose included their classrooms, private offices at their schools, or their homes. I also explained to them prior to the interview what the focus of the interview was and how long I foresaw the interview lasting. I invited the teachers to generate their own questions and/or to include any information they wanted. I also made it clear that what they discussed with me was confidential and that they could end the interview at any point they wanted. For this purpose, all teacher and school names that appear in this book are pseudonyms.

INFORMAL INTERVIEWS

In contrast to formal interviews, informal interviews are much more open-ended, spontaneous, and casual. In many ways the informal interview resembles a casual conversation. Spradley (1979) points out that when researchers conduct informal interviews, "They [researchers] may interview people without their awareness, merely carrying on a friendly conversation while introducing a few ethnographic questions" (p. 58). So the informal interviews are casual in that they are not scheduled, can occur anytime or any place (e.g., during recess on a playground), and are intermixed with friendly conversation. That is not to say, however, that informal interviews have no structure whatsoever. In an informal interview, the researcher has specific questions in mind and carefully guides the conversation so that the participant may address those specific questions.

Further, informal interviews not only serve as an efficient way to collect data, but also to verify data that was collected through other means. As such, informal interviews both provided me the opportunity to gather information I was not aware of and to verify data I had collected from other methods. In the latter case, for example, informal interviews can be used to clarify any ambiguities in data already collected. In the case of Ms. DeGraw, I verified data I collected during a participant-observation I conducted through the use of an informal interview. The initial data collection occurred during a participant-observation session when Mrs. Short (ESL counselor) visited Ms. DeGraw's class and talked to the students about college and jobs. Mrs. Short discussed with the students:

Mrs. Short: It is not necessary to get a college degree in order to make a lot of money. Take my husband, for example. He never got a college degree. He opened up a business and makes good money.

Upon hearing this, Ms. DeGraw leaned over to me and told me in a soft voice:

Ms. DeGraw: See! That's just wrong.

When Ms. DeGraw told me this I assumed she was referring to Mrs. Short's de-emphasis of a college education. However, I was not positive, so I made a note to ask Ms. DeGraw about this at a later point. Later that day when we were both cleaning up the classroom, I engaged Ms. DeGraw in an informal interview. After some small talk, I asked Ms. DeGraw what she meant by the comment she told me during Mrs. Short's lesson. Ms. DeGraw then elaborated:

Ms. DeGraw: It's just wrong that she [Mrs. Short] gets to talk about her husband at school. She is completely oblivious that I cannot talk about my partner here. She simply doesn't recognize the privilege she has and exercises every day.

In this informal interview I learned that Ms. DeGraw was talking about the silencing of gay and lesbian faculty on the job as well as the privileging of straight people, instead of the de-emphasis of a college education for her ESL students. As can be seen, it was critical that I follow up and verify these data in an informal interview in order to avoid drastically misrepresenting Ms. DeGraw's comment. An informal interview was the only efficient way to verify these data as it allowed me to ask a specific question in a timely manner. If I had saved this question for the next scheduled formal interview, Ms. DeGraw would have likely either forgotten making the statement or the meaning behind the statement.

DATA ANALYSIS

As I analyzed all the data sources, I utilized the constant comparative method (Strauss, 1996), in which I continually analyzed data for emerging patterns or themes. This involved an inductive data analysis (Crenshaw, 2014) process in that I analyzed data as I collected it so that I could begin to identify patterns in the data. As mentioned above in the participant-observation section, I had to make decisions about what to attend to while in the process of taking field notes. It would be impossible to record everything in the site that registered my senses. The process of deciding what about the field site could potentially be relevant to my research, whether explicit or not, involved an on-site analysis of the data as it was being collected. I also mentioned in my discussions on interviews that it was important that I listen and analyze what the participants were saying during their interviews, so that I could make decisions on whether the information could potentially emerge as a theme, and thus whether it deserved further attention such as a follow-up question. This process also involved continual data analysis.

Once the data took the form of written texts such as field notes and interview transcripts, I began a more systematic process in which I coded and recoded (Auerbach & Silverstein, 2003; Flick, 2014) data for themes. When certain themes emerged from the data, I further analyzed the data through the triangulation method (Flick, 2014), in which I compared and verified themes through three different informational sources including participant-observations, formal interviews, and informal interviews. Triangulation was not used as a means to achieve coherency, validity, or generalizability (Eisner, 2017) but rather to construct case studies that closely approximate the participants' lived experiences. Undoubtedly, through the data collection process, I obtained a rich sense of who the teachers were and a detailed understanding of the school settings in which they were teaching. For an introduction and overview of each teacher and school, please refer to the individual case-study chapters.

REFERENCES

Alemán, Jr. E. (Producer), & Luna, L. (Director). (2013). *Stolen education* [Documentary]. Salt Lake City, UT: Alemán/Luna Productions.

Auerbach, C. F., & Silverstein, L. B. (2003). *Qualitative data*. New York, NY: New York University Press.

Banks, J. A., & McGee, B. C. A. (2013). *Multicultural education: Issues and perspectives*. Hoboken, NJ: John Wiley & Sons, Inc.

Bell, D. (1980). Brown v. board of education and the interest-convergence dilemma. *Harvard Law Review, 93*(3), 518–534.

Bomer, R., Dworin, J. E., May, L., & Semingson, P. (2008). Miseducating teachers about the poor: A critical analysis of Ruby Payne's claims about poverty. *Teachers College Record, 110*(12), 2497–2531.

Bonilla-Silva, E. (2014). *Racism without racists: Color-blind racism and racial inequality in contemporary America*. Lanham, MD: Rowman & Littlefield Publishers.

Bonilla-Silva, E., & Dietrich, D. (2011). The sweet enchantment of color-blind racism in Obamerica. *The ANNALS of the American Academy of Political and Social Science, 634*(1), 190–206.

Brinkmann, S., & Kvale, S. (2015). *Interviews: Learning the craft of qualitative research interviewing*. Thousand Oaks, CA: Sage.

Britzman, D. P. (2003). *Practice makes practice: A critical study of learning to teach*. New York, NY: State University of New York.

Buendía, E. (2000). Power and possibility: The construction of a pedagogical practice. *Teaching and Teacher Education, 16*, 147–163.

Buendía, E., Gitlin, A., & Doumbia, F. (2003). Working the pedagogical borderlands: An African critical pedagogue teaching within an assimilationist context. *Curriculum Inquiry, 33*, 291–320.

Cammarota, J. (2011). Blindsided by the avatar: White saviors and allies out of Hollywood and in education. *The Review of Education, Pedagogy, and Cultural Studies, 33*(3), 242–259.

Cammarota, J. (2016). Social Justice Education Project (SJEP): A case example of PAR in a high school classroom. In A. Valenzuela (Ed.), *Growing critically conscious teachers: A social justice curriculum for educators of Latino/a youth* (pp. 90–104). New York, NY: Teachers College Press.

Carter, R. T. (1995). *The influence of race and racial identity in psychotherapy: Towards a racially inclusive model*. New York, NY: Wiley.

Charmaz, K. (2014). *Constructing grounded theory*. Thousand Oakes, CA: Sage.

Cowey, M. (2006). *Black ants and Buddhists: Thinking critically and teaching differently in the primary grades*. Portland, MA: Stenhouse.

Crenshaw, J. W. (2014). *Research design: Qualitative, quantitative, and mixed method approaches*. Thousand Oaks, CA: Sage.

Cummins, J. (1996). *Negotiating identities: Education for empowerment in a diverse society*. CA: Ontario: California Association for Bilingual Education.

Darling-Hammond, L. (2010). *The flat world and education: How America's commitment to equity will determine our future*. New York, NY: Teachers College Press.

DiAngelo, R. (2011). White fragility. *International Journal of Critical Pedagogy, 3*, 54–70.

Delpit, L. (2012). *"Multiplication is for White people": Raising expectations for other people's children*. New York, NY: The New Press.

Dunn, A. H., Dotson, E. K., Ford, J. C., & Roberts, M. A. (2014). "You won't believe what they said in class today": Professors' reflections on student resistance in multicultural education courses. *Multicultural Perspectives, 16*(2), 93–98.

Education Week. (2013). *Baltimore leader helps district cut suspensions*. Retrieved from http://www.edweek.org/ew/articles/2013/02/06/20ltlf-brice.h32.html

Eisner, E. (2017). *The enlightened eye: Qualitative inquiry and the enhancement of educational practice*. New York, NY: Teachers College Press.

REFERENCES

Emerson, R. M., Fretz, R. I., & Shaw, L. L. (2011). *Writing ethnographic fieldnotes.* Chicago, IL: The University of Chicago Press.

Fetterman, D. M. (2010). *Ethnography: Step-by-step.* Thousand Oaks, CA: Sage.

Flick, U. (2014). *An introduction to qualitative research.* Los Angeles, CA: Sage.

Flynn, J. E., (2015). White fatigue: Naming the challenge in moving from an individual to a systemic understanding of racism. *Multicultural Perspectives, 17*(3), 115–124.

Foucault, M. (1981). *The history of sexuality, Volume. one: An introduction.* Harmondsworth, NY: Pelican.

Freeman, Y. S., Freeman, D. E., & Mercuri, S. P. (2004). *Dual language essentials for teachers and administrators.* Portsmouth, NH: Heinemann.

Freire, P. (1985). *The politics of education: Culture, power, and liberation.* South Hadley, MA: Bergen & Garvey.

Freire, P. (2000). *Pedagogy of the oppressed.* New York, NY: Bloomsbury.

Gándara, P., & Contreras, F. (2010). *The Latino education crisis: The consequences of failed social policies.* Cambridge, MA: Harvard University Press.

Gay, G. (2010). *Culturally responsive teaching: Theory, research, and practice.* New York, NY: Teachers College Press.

Ginwright, S., & Cammarota, J. (2011). Youth organizing in the wild west: mobilizing for educational justice in Arizona! *Voices in Urban Education, 30*, 13–21.

Hamayan, E., Genesee, F., & Cloud, N. (2013). *Dual language instruction from a to z: Practical guidance for teachers and administrators.* Portsmouth, NH: Heinemann.

Haviland, V. S. (2008). "Things get glossed over": Rearticulating the silencing power of Whiteness in education. *Journal of Teacher Education, 59*(1), 40–54.

Helms, J. E. (1992). *A race is a nice thing to have: A guide to being a White person or understanding the White persons in your life.* Topeka, KS: Content Communications.

Howard, G. R. (2006). *We can't teach what we don't know: White teachers, multiracial schools.* New York, NY: Teachers College Press.

Intercultural Development Research Association. (2015, October 29). *30th annual Texas public school attrition study.* Retrieved from http://nces.ed.gov/programs/digest/d13/tables/dt13_203.50.asp

Jones, S. P. (2015). *Blame teachers: The emotional reasons for educational reform.* Charlotte, NY: Information Age Publishing.

Kayne, E. (2013, June 13). Census: White majority in U.S. gone by 2043. *NBC News.* Retrieved from http://usnews.nbcnews.com/_news/2013/06/13/18934111-census-white-majority-in-us-gone-by-2043?lite

Kozol, J. (1991). *Savage inequalities: Children in America's schools.* New York, NY: Crown Publishers.

Kozol, J. (2005). *The shame of the nation: The restoration of apartheid schooling in America.* New York, NY: Crown Publishers.

Ladson-Billings, G. (2001). *Crossing over to canaan: The journey of new teachers in diverse classrooms.* San Francisco, CA: Jossey-Bass.

Ladson-Billings, G. (2009). *The dream-keepers: Successful teachers of African American children.* San Francisco, CA: Jossey-Bass.

LaDuke, A. E. (2009). Resistance and renegotiation: Preservice teacher interactions with and reactions to multicultural course content. *Multicultural Education, 16*(3), 37–44.

Laura, C. T. (2014). *Being bad: My baby brother and the school-to-prison pipeline.* New York, NY: Teachers College Press.

Lawrence, S. M., & Tatum, B. D. (1997). White teachers as allies: Moving from awareness to action. In M. Fine, L. Weis, L. C. Powell, & L. M. Wong (Eds.), *Off White: Readings on race, power, and society* (pp. 333–342). New York, NY: Routledge.

Lee, E., Menkart, D., & Okazawa-Rey, M. (Eds.). (2008). *Beyond heroes and holidays: A practical guide to k-12 anti-racist, multicultural education and staff development.* Washington, DC: Teaching for Change.

Lewin, T. (2012, March 6). Black students face more discipline, data suggest. *The New York Times.* Retrieved from http://www.nytimes.com/2012/03/06/education/black-students-face-more-harsh-discipline-data-shows.html?_r=0Lyfe

Lindholm-Leary, K. J. (2001). *Dual language education*. Clevedon: Multilingual Matters.

Mercado, C. I. (2016). Teacher capacities for Latino and Latina youth. In A. Valenzuela (Ed.), *Growing critically conscious teachers: A social justice curriculum for educators of Latino/a youth* (pp. 24–38). New York, NY: Teachers College Press.

Michie, G. (2005). *See you when we get there: Teaching for change in urban schools*. New York, NY: Teachers College Press.

Michie, G. (2009). *Holler if you hear me: The education of a teacher and his students*. New York, NY: Teachers College Press.

Milner, H. R. (2010). *Start where you are, but don't stay there*. Cambridge, MA: Harvard Education Press.

Milner, H. R. (2015). *Rac(e)ing to class: Confronting poverty and race in schools and classrooms*. Cambridge, MA: Harvard Education Press.

National Center for Education Statistics. (2013). Retrieved from http://nces.ed.gov/programs/digest/d13/tables/dt13_209.10.asp

National Educational Association. (2005). Retrieved from http://www.nea.org/home/13598.htm

Nieto, S. (2010). *The light in their eyes: Creating multicultural learning communities*. New York, NY: Teachers College Press.

Nieto, S. (2017). Re-imagining multicultural education: New visions, new possibilities. *Multicultural Education Review, 9*(1), 1–10.

Nieto, S., & Bode, P. (2012). *Affirming diversity: The sociopolitical context of multicultural education*. Boston, MA: Pearson.

Orfield, G. (2008). *Race and schools: The need for action* (Research Brief: 1b). Washington, DC: National Education Association. Retrieved from http://www.nea.org/home/13054.htm

Payne, R. K. (2005). *A framework for understanding poverty*. Highlands, TE: Aha Process Inc.

Pimentel, C. (2011). The color of language: The racialized educational trajectory of an emerging bilingual student. *Journal of Latinos and Education, 10*(4), 1–19.

Ramsey, P. G. (2015). *Teaching and learning in a diverse world: Multicultural education for young children*. New York, NY: Teachers College Press.

Shuck, G. (2006). Racializing the nonnative English speaker. *Journal of Language, Identity, and Education, 5*(4), 259–276.

Sleeter, C. E. (1992). *Keepers of the American dream*. Bristol, PA: The Falmer Press.

Sleeter, C. E. (2015). *White bread: Weaving cultural past into the present*. Boston, MA: Sense Publishers.

Sleeter, C. E., & Grant, C. A. (2009). *Making choices for multicultural education: Five approaches to race, class, and gender*. New York, NY: John Wiley & Sons, Inc.

Spradley, J. P. (1979). *The ethnographic interview*. Fort Worth, TX: Harcourt Brace Jovanovich College Publishers.

Spradley, J. P. (1980). *Participant observation*. Orlando, FL: Harcourt Brace College Publishers.

Strauss, A. L. (1996). *Qualitative analysis for social scientists*. New York, NY: Cambridge University Press.

Strom, K. J., & Martin, A. D. (2017). *Becoming-teacher: A rhizomatic look at first-year teaching*. Rotterdam: Sense Publishers.

Tatum, B. D. (2014). Defining racism: "Can we talk". In G. B. Rodman (Ed.), *The race reader* (pp. 25–32). New York, NY: Routledge.

Texas Education Agency. (2014). *Enrollment in Texas public schools 2013–2014*. Austin, TE: Division of Research and Analysis, Department of Assessment and Accountability.

Thompson, A. (1997). Political pragmatism and educational inquiry. In F. Margonis (Ed.), *Philosophy of education: 1996* (pp. 425–434). Urbana, IL: Philosophy of Education Society.

Thompson, A. (1999). Colortalk: Whiteness and off White. *Educational Studies, 30*, 141–160.

Twine, F. W. (2010). *A White side of Black Britain: Interrracial intimacy and racial literacy*. Durham, NC: Duke University Press.

Urrieta, L. Jr. (2009). *Working from within: Chicana and Chicano activist educators in White stream schools*. Tucson, AZ: The University of Arizona Press.

REFERENCES

Valencia, R. R. (2011). The plight of Chicano students: An overview of schooling conditions and outcomes. In R. R. Valencia (Ed.), *Chicano school failure and success: Past, present, and future* (pp. 3–41). New York, NY: Routledge.

Valencia, R. R. (2015). *Students of color and the achievement gap: Systemic challenges, systemic transformations.* New York, NY: Routledge.

Valencia, R. R., & Solórzano, D. (2004). Today's deficit thinking about the education of minority students. In O. S. Ana (Ed.), *Tongue-tied: The lives of multilingual children in public education* (pp. 124–133). Lanham, MD: Rowman & Littlefield Publishers.

Valenzuela, A. (1999). *Subtractive schooling: U.S. Mexican youth and the politics of caring.* New York, NY: State University of New York Press.

Villanueva, V. (1993). *Bootstraps: From an American academic of color.* Urbana, IL: National Council of Teachers of English.

Wise, T. (2010). *Colorblind: The rise of post racial politics and the retreat from racial equity.* San Francisco, CA: City Lights Publishers.

Yin, R. K. (2014). *Case study research: Design and methods.* Thousand Oaks, CA: Sage.

Yosso, T. J. (2006). *Critical race counterstories along the Chicana/Chicano educational pipeline.* New York, NY: Routledge.

Yosso, T., & Solórzano, D. (2006). Leaks in the Chicana and Chicano educational pipeline. *Latino Policy & Issues Brief, 13,* 1–4.

INDEX

CPSIA information can be obtained
at www.ICGtesting.com
Printed in the USA
LVOW05s0143230817

545974LV00008B/88/P